The Changing Business of Journalism and its Implications for Democracy

Edited by David A. L. Levy
and Rasmus Kleis Nielsen

REUTERS
INSTITUTE for the
STUDY of
JOURNALISM

398442

Contents

Executive summary

The business of journalism is widely held to be in serious crisis today, in particular because of the rise of the internet. This has potentially disastrous consequences for forms of democratic politics that have evolved hand-in-hand with private-sector mass media as we have known them in the twentieth century. This book includes chapters from around the world critically evaluating the notion of crisis, identifying both the common underlying cyclical, technological and long-term challenges that commercial news media organisations around the world face *and* the important, persistent national differences in audience demand, market structure and media regulation that suggest different likely future scenarios for different countries.

While the news industry has certainly suffered severe declines in revenues in several countries in recent years, the latest downturns seem to be more closely connected with the relative degree of dependence on volatile revenue sources like advertising and on the differential impact of the global recession than with the spread of the internet. This is illustrated perhaps most forcefully by the difference between countries like the United States and the United Kingdom, where the private media sector have struggled in recent years, whereas countries like Germany and Finland – with comparable levels of internet penetration and use and strong public service media organisations operating on several platforms – have seen much more stable developments in the business of journalism. Both the news industry and the journalistic profession are changing rapidly as new tools are being appropriated by journalists, sources and audiences, but the supposed crisis is far from universal, and the outcomes of current transformations far from certain.

The differences identified and documented in this book not only highlight the enduring relevance of inherited national differences in audience demand, market structure and media regulation, but also that, despite deterministic (and often fatalistic) claims to the contrary, there is still time for the business of journalism to reinvent itself and move into the twenty-first century, provided media managers, professional journalists, and policy-makers and the citizens they represent are willing to learn from different developments around the world.

The value of the chapters to follow lies in their detailed assessment of particular challenges or cases, and we will not attempt to summarise them here, but simply highlight a few particularly important points from each. In Chapter 1, Rasmus Kleis Nielsen and David A. L. Levy present a wide array of data to establish that different national media systems are developing very differently even as legacy media face comparable cyclical, technological and long-term challenges. In Chapter 2, Robert G. Picard reminds us that general interest news never was a profitable business in itself, but always cross-subsidised by other interests, whether commercial or political. In Chapter 3, Sacha Wunsch-Vincent reviews recent technological developments to show how new information and communications technologies have changed the value chain of news businesses, how journalists work, how audiences use news, and how they are increasingly transforming the wider communications environment as new players like aggregators and search engines rise to prominence. In Chapter 4, Frank Esser and Michael Brüggemann show how well the German media system has withstood current pressures, and argue that, in so far as there are any signs of crisis there, it is not a crisis for democracy or journalism in general, but at most a strategic crisis for newspapers in particular. In Chapter 5, Hannu Nieminen presents an overview of developments in Finland, where most commercial legacy media organisations also seem to have weathered the storm relatively well, despite high levels of internet penetration and use and the presence of a strong public service media organisation in YLE. However, Nieminen points out, the post-war media policy consensus within which this apparently sturdy media system developed may now be unravelling. In Chapter 6, Alice Antheaume underlines that crisis is nothing new in the French press, still constrained by systems of distribution and production developed to deal with post-Second World War shortages and never subsequently reformed, systems that today leave the newspaper industry in perennial crisis and reliant on periodic bailouts by the state. In Chapter 7, John Lloyd reviews the situation in the United Kingdom, discusses the extent to which new forms of peer-to-peer production can make up for what is lost when inherited forms of journalistic work are displaced or destroyed, and underlines the enduring relevance of traditional news journalism. In Chapter 8, Michael Schudson reflects upon the case of the United States, where the current crisis has hit first – and hardest – and sketches out likely scenarios for the immediate future and their democratic implications. Chapters 9 and 10 turn the focus to the business of journalism in two emerging economies where the picture looks rather different. In Chapter 9, Mauro P. Porto underlines not only how the Brazilian media are still struggling with debt acquired during the 1990s, but also how many parts of the sector, in particular TV but also the press, are now profiting from sustained economic growth, increasing literacy, and declining poverty. In Chapter 10, Daya Kishan Thussu shows how dramatically the Indian media have grown since the sector was liberalised in the 1990s, but also how most of the content produced is largely 'Bollywoodized', focusing on entertainment and sensational soft news rather than hard news covering public affairs. In Chapter 11, Rasmus Kleis Nielsen and David A. L. Levy write about current policy discussions; they underline the need to take into account the widely different situations the media industry in general and the business of journalism in particular face in different countries – even when confronted with comparable challenges – but also the need for national policy-makers to look beyond their traditional national policy toolkits.

1. The Changing Business of Journalism and its Implications for Democracy

Rasmus Kleis Nielsen and David A. L. Levy

Introduction

Journalism and democracy are intimately connected. All around the world, people can quote their own favourite founding father, prominent publisher or inspiring intellectual to that effect. What kind of journalism we prefer, what kind of democracy we want and what we make of the connection – all that we might disagree over, but the two are intertwined for good and for bad, and a change in one will have implications for the other.

Today, journalism is changing, partly because of changes in the business that sustains – and sometimes constrains – it. The changing business of journalism is the subject of this book, which we have put together because we believe that the changes afoot in the industry have implications that go well beyond it, and that cross-national comparative perspectives such as those presented here can help us break the narrowly national frame within which contemporary changes in journalism are often discussed. Each of our contributors deals in detail with recent developments in journalism, focusing on a shared challenge or a single country. In combination, they offer a multi-faceted analysis of the situation of the business of journalism in different settings, and how it is changing.

People today access news in many different ways, using many different media platforms – ranging from the inherited trio of print, radio, and television to various internet and mobile applications. But this diversity of platforms aside, the majority of professionally produced news journalism is in most countries still primarily underwritten by newspapers (Pew Project for Excellence in Journalism 2010a; Lund *et al.* 2009) – or what we should today probably call something like 'multi-media news organisations with a particular emphasis on print', as they have moved online and started offering interactive graphics, podcasts, video streaming, and the like. Newspapers are particularly central in the United States, where the three national television networks in 2009 employed only about 500 journalists, and the number of journalists working full-time for non-profit and online-only operations remains limited, whereas the newspaper industry – even after often brutal staff cuts in 2007 and

2008 – employed more than 40,000 full-time journalists (Pew Project for Excellence in Journalism 2010b). But it is also true in, for example, the United Kingdom, home of the BBC, the largest and most well-known public service media organisation in the world. Whereas 'the Beeb' employs about 7,000 journalists around the world, the private press employs more than 12,000 (see Davis 2002, for estimates of the national press; WAN 2009, for data on regional/local press).

We thus pay particular attention to commercial legacy news media organisations here – especially to newspapers as they operate on and offline – because they generally constitute the largest part of the business of journalism, underwrite most of the professionally produced news content people peruse around the world, and are undergoing sometimes dramatic change today. Our focus does not imply that public service media organisations, non-profit and community media, and new online-only ventures do not also have an important role to play in our expanding communications environment, but simply that the private news industry remains of absolutely central importance for the future of journalism.

Commercial legacy news organisations engaged in the business of journalism confront three kinds of challenges today, and in this introduction we will present a brief overview of the forms they take in different countries. First, they face a *cyclical downturn* in advertising caused by the global financial crisis of 2008–9. Second, they face increased competition for attention and advertisements and a new environment due to the rise of a range of *new technologies* stretching from cable and satellite television in the 1970s and 1980s to the dramatic rise of the internet from the 1990s onwards. Third, they continue to face challenges rooted in *long-term changes* of a political, social, and economic character.

Many have prophesied that these challenges – the internet in particular – will kill the newspaper and thus fundamentally transform journalism as we have known it in the twentieth century. We disagree with this view. We do not believe that the internet will prevent newspapers and other commercial news organisations from making privately profitable and potentially publicly valuable contributions to our democracies. The recession has hurt journalism as an occupation (they tend to). New technologies will change how journalists practise their trade and how the business of journalism is conducted (they often do). Longer term political, social, and economic developments will eventually change the wider media industry (they always do). But there is no evidence to support the claim that there is one determinate end-point for the developments that the business of journalism is going through today, let alone for the assertion that current changes signal the end of commercial news organisations as such.

Our media systems are today in the early stages of what will be a great transformation, partially driven by a wide range of new technologies that have unleashed gales of what the political economist Joseph Schumpeter once called 'creative destruction'. As media markets readjust, journalists' work changes towards distributed forms of temporary and project-based employment, and citizens access, use, and generate content in new ways, the consequences will be profound and probably often painful for thousands of individual journalists who will lose their jobs or see their vocation transformed. Yet while the business of journalism is changing, and in some countries shrinking, it does not seem to be going away. If you find yourself in France believing the claim that the internet has killed the newspaper, take a look at Finland, where high internet penetration coexists with high newspaper circulation. If you hear in the United

Kingdom that free public service media content is what undermines the ability of commercial news organisations to make money online, take a look at the United States, where newspapers and private television and radio channels face little competition from public service media organisations, and yet struggle to find an online business model.

Even a cursory look at the seven countries dealt with in the rest of the book – Germany, Finland, France, the United Kingdom, the United States, Brazil, and India – suggests that the state of the business of journalism is highly diverse today, even among countries with otherwise comparable levels of economic, technological, and social and political development. Even if everything else was equal, the consequences of the 2008–9 recession were always going to be more severe in an American newspaper sector that gets on average about 87 per cent of its revenue from advertising than it has been in Germany or Finland, where newspapers get, respectively, 53 and 54 per cent of their revenue from advertising and the rest from sales (OECD 2010).

To get a better grasp of these variations, we have asked our wide range of contributors to provide us with an overview of the situation in countries they know well. The case countries included in this book represent examples of what media researchers Daniel C. Hallin and Paolo Mancini (2004) have characterised as 'liberal' media systems (the United States, the United Kingdom), 'democratic corporatist' media systems (Finland, Germany), 'polarised pluralist' media systems (France and to some extent Brazil), but also a country that seems to fall partially or entirely outside this established framework for comparative media research (India). The countries discussed here represent a wide range of different media systems, sometimes with lessons from one relevant for understanding others. To preface our contributors' detailed discussions in later chapters, let us offer here a brief overview of the main similarities and differences in the cyclical, technological, and long-term challenges the business of journalism faces across the world.

Cyclical challenges

The global financial crisis of 2008–9 was accompanied by what was in many developed democracies the worst recession in the post-war period. The impact was immediate and often severe for commercial news media organisations around the world, but also very different from country to country. Figure 1.1 presents the OECD's estimates of revenue change in newspaper publishing in various countries (including advertisements, sales, and other sources of income). The numbers were dramatic in countries like the United States (-30%) and the United Kingdom (-21%), but much more modest in many other developed democracies like Germany (-10%), Finland (-7%) and, most notably, France (-4%).

In many countries, the financial crisis – in some cases further exacerbated by domestic recessions, housing slumps, and other related downturns – led to stagnation in total advertisement expenditures, and in a few cases to actual decreases. The World Advertising Research Centre (WARC) estimates that total advertising expenditure declined by 6.3 per cent from 2007 to 2008 in the United States, and by a dramatic 10.4 per cent in the United Kingdom – a serious challenge for any advertising-dependent media organisation, whether an online start-up, a free-to-air television station, or a newspaper. But the same year saw growth in other mature markets like Germany (6.8%) and France (6.4%), and continued high-level growth in emerging markets like Brazil (20.3%) and India (19.3%). (See Table 1.1.)

5

Figure 1.1. Estimated change in total newspaper publishing revenues (2007-9)

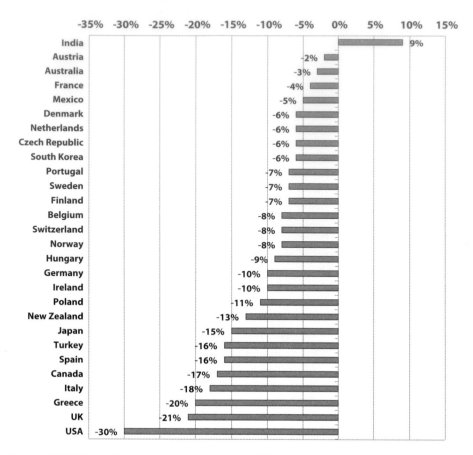

Data from OECD (2010) with additional data from PricewaterhouseCoopers (2010).

Table 1.1. Total advertising expenditures, top ten countries plus India and Finland (2007-2008)

Country	2007 (current US$m)	2008 (current US$m)	year-on-year change
USA	169,178	158,547	-6.3%
China	44,805	75,077	27.4%
Japan	38,529	41,902	8.8%
Germany	26,759	28,569	6.8%
United Kingdom	29,911	26,802	-10.4%
France	16,031	17,062	6.4%
Italy	12,844	13,501	5.1%
Canada	11,270	11,836	5.0%
Brazil	9,509	11,440	20.3%
Australia	10,664	11,254	5.5%
India	6,305	7,524	19.3%
Finland	2,073	2,261	9.1%

Data from WARC (2009) on top ten countries, India and Finland added from WARC. For comparative purposes, the data are shown in US$. Exchange rate fluctuations can distort annual growth.

Total advertising expenditure is widely expected to grow strongly around the world as the wider economy recovers (as happened in the years after the dot.com bubble burst and after previous recessions). Though commercial news organisations in general and newspapers in particular capture only a part of total advertisement expenditures – and in many countries a shrinking part, relatively speaking – renewed growth in advertising is in general good news for the business of journalism. While it is uncertain whether we should expect to see such a situation again in the near future, it is worth keeping in mind that in 2006-7 – before the global financial crisis, but more than ten years after graphical web browsers like Mosaic and the spread of dial-up modems started making the internet accessible to a wider audience and after decades of declining circulation – newspapers were very profitable businesses in many countries. The average operating surplus amongst the 27 European Union member states was 11 per cent, and operating profits in American newspapers often at 20 per cent or more (Pew Project for Excellence in Journalism 2010). (See Figure 1.2.)

Figure 1.2. Gross operating surplus in newspaper publishing (2007)

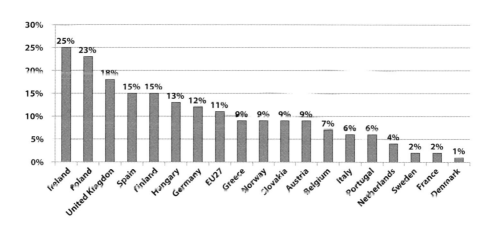

Data from OECD (2010); data for Ireland, Finland, UK, EU27, Greece, Norway, and France are from 2006.

Technological challenges

The first decade of the twenty-first century has seen the rapid spread of increasingly sophisticated forms of internet access and use throughout the developed world and in many emerging economies. Well into the 1990s, many central and southern European countries lagged behind the Anglophone world and Northern Europe in terms of internet penetration, but the late 2000s have seen trends towards convergence around similarly high levels of use across the developed world, often at 70 per cent or more. (See Figure 1.3.) While variations in access and use correlated with class, education, gender, and in some cases race, generally persist, the internet is today undoubtedly a mass phenomenon.

Both legacy (print, radio, television) and new (so-called 'pure player') media organisations offer news online today. Along with the breakdown of old broadcasting

Figure 1.3. Internet users per 1,000 population (1999–2009)

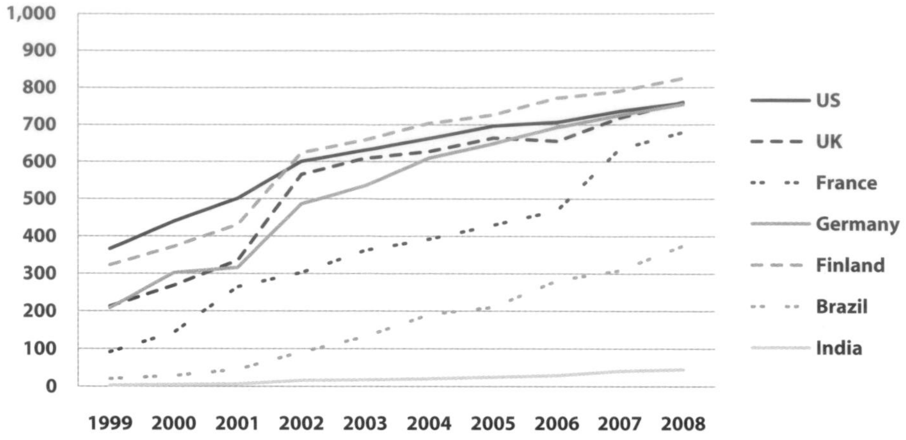

Data from the World Bank.

monopolies, the spread of cable and satellite television, and the rise of free dailies in many urban areas, the move online has increased competition for audience attention and advertising expenditures, in particular amongst the younger affluent consumers who are most attractive to advertisers and who are often also early adopters and heavy users of new media technologies. The internet and new mobile technologies have thus not only helped change the very nature of news consumption for many people, transformed the everyday work routines of journalists, and facilitated an increasingly accelerated news cycle with 24/7 updating and commentary. They have also brought a wide range of historically distinct media organisations head-to-head in competition for the same potential users.

News remains a small part of all online traffic – far smaller than search, social networking, and various forms of entertainment (data from Experian Hitwise suggests news amounts to about 4.4 per cent of United States internet traffic in 2010, a somewhat higher 6.7 per cent in the United Kingdom, but only 3.3 per cent in France). There are major cross-national variations not only in terms of the absolute and relative volume of traffic, but also in terms of where people find their news online. In the United States, aggregators like Yahoo! News and Google News attract large numbers of visitors, and several pure players (like the *Drudge Report* and the *Huffington Post*) play prominent roles, whereas legacy organisations, whether public service media organisations like the BBC or private newspapers or news-magazines like *Le Monde* or *Der Spiegel*, often play a leading role in online news provision in European countries.

While there are examples of individual commercial news organisations who run what seem to be sustainable online business models, the wider news industry is still searching for a generalisable model for commercially sustainable online news production. Internet advertising is a growing share of a growing market in most countries, but the massive supply of display advertising in particular means that it continues to be virtually impossible for commercial legacy news organisations to generate the same kind of revenue per reader or viewer that they have been accustomed to on print or via broadcasting. The business of journalism is therefore still overwhelmingly based on revenue from inherited media platforms. Both print and broadcast attract large but widely different percentages of (equally widely different) overall advertising expenditures from country to country (see Figure 1.4). Germany, the United Kingdom, and the United States, for example, have almost identical levels of broadband penetration (and Germany and the UK have comparable per capita newspaper circulation), but the distribution of advertising revenue is very different. Internet sites attract 15 per cent of all advertisement expenditures in Germany, but 23 per cent in the United Kingdom and 15 per cent in the United States, whereas newspapers attract 37 per cent in Germany, compared to 28 and 22 per cent in the United Kingdom and the United States respectively.[1]

Figure 1.4. Distribution of advertising expenditures (2008)

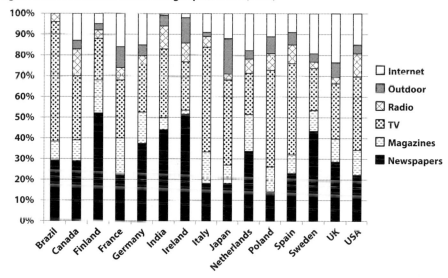

Data from Ofcom (2009) and WARC (2008). Data for Brazil, Finland, and India from 2007.
Please note that WARC data is used rather than national sources to allow for consistent comparison.

Long-term challenges

Contemporary debates often focus only on the cyclical and technological challenges outlined above, and fail to acknowledge that many current trends in the business of journalism are continuations of decades-old political, social, and economic developments.

Politically, today's news industry operates in an environment shaped by years of deregulation, in particular in the United States, where historical cross-media ownership regulations were weakened by the Telecommunication Act of 1996. In Europe the direction of travel is similar even if the outcomes are more uncertain. The European Commission has recognised the right of member states to fund public service media organisations and to some extent to directly and indirectly subsidise the press (Ward 2003). However, pressures towards market liberalisation, reduced or more rigorously policed subsidies, and the removal of barriers to a single European market have been driven in part by Commission attempts to reform state aid provisions for the media

---

[1] The British and American percentages come from a proportionally larger total advertisement market. Whereas the USA, the UK, and Germany had roughly comparable current $ GDP per capita in 2008, advertisements amounted to 1.9% of GDP in the USA versus 0.85% in the UK and 0.76% in Germany (WARC 2008).

sector. This in turn has been prompted largely by the number of complaints lodged in Brussels by industry players and their lobby groups. These groups often see Brussels as offering them their best chance of reining in the ambitions of publicly funded media organisations. At the national level, commercial media companies often argue for the removal of some forms of sector-specific media regulation as a requirement for survival or the precondition for the creation of 'national champions' that can see off the threat posed by international – predominantly US-based – competitors.

In some countries, these developments have led to consolidation and sometimes increased concentration in the media industry. Many commentators worry about the consequences (Baker 2002) and, in both the United States and Europe, media reform movements have warned against current developments and called for renewed regulation and new forms of public intervention. However, the tendency towards concentration has also, on occasion, increased the countervailing power that media companies themselves exercise over the policy process, as politicians fear the consequences of defying powerful media conglomerates.

Most European countries continue to operate public service media organisations at least partially funded by licence fees and with some obligation to provide general interest news (and often with very substantial audience shares), thus reducing their relative systemic dependency on commercial media in general and private newspapers in particular for news production and diffusion. Many European countries, in particular in Scandinavia and around the Mediterranean, have historically in addition offered direct state subsidies to the private press to sustain the industry and/or ensure media pluralism in both national and local markets. The balance between general subsidies to the entire industry (often given to support production and/or distribution) and more targeted subsidies to, for example, second newspapers in two-newspaper towns, or to political and ideological publications with a limited advertising base, differs from country to country (Fernández Alonso 2006). While licence fees remain in place in many countries and indirect subsidies for much of the wider media sector exist everywhere, direct subsidies to the press have generally been reduced in recent years. Table 1.2 offers a brief overview of state funding for direct press subsidies and for public service media organisations (and their reach) for a range of European countries and the United States. As can be seen, direct press subsidies, where they exist, are very limited compared to licence fees.

Socially, many contemporary media systems are less and less dominated by a few archetypical mass media like nation-wide free-to-air broadcasters (public or private) and general interest newspapers (national or regional). Most trends point towards increasingly fragmented communications environments characterised by higher

Table 1.2. Public funding for direct press subsidies and public service (2008)

	Direct Press Subsidies (€ per capita)	PSMO Funding (€ per capita)	Public Service TV Share of All Viewing
Finland	0.09	72.00	45%
France	1.48	46.54	36%
Germany	0.00	86.79	31%
UK	0.00	70.44	37%
US	0.00	1.25	1%

Data from OfCom (2009) YLE (2008), WAN (2009). Currencies compared at annual average exchange rate.

levels of consumer choice, more volatile (and sometimes engaged) audiences, and many competing providers of both news and entertainment operating across several platforms – most commercial, but some public, and a few based on communities of interest or new forms of peer-production. In many countries, television use is still high but increasingly segmented, and paid newspaper circulation declining, in particular amongst younger cohorts (the rise of free dailies has partially or fully counterbalanced this in terms of overall circulation in some countries). (See Figure 1.5.) It is important to note, however, that many of these social changes in how news is accessed have been underway for years, with newspaper circulation peaking in many countries as early as the 1960s (or even before) and falling ever since, just as the audience share of individual broadcasters has been declining across the world since the end of monopoly, generally in the 1970s and 1980s, and the rise of cable and satellite television in the 1990s.

Figure 1.5. Newspaper circulation per 1,000 population (2000–2009)

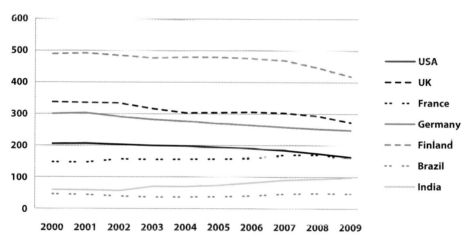

Data from WAN (2009) and the World Bank.

Economically, today's news industry continues to be structured very differently from country to country. Indeed, the countries classified by media researchers as having 'liberal', 'democratic corporatist', and 'polarised pluralist' media systems (Hallin and Mancini 2004) to a high degree correspond to countries with what comparative political economists call 'liberal market economies', 'coordinated market economies', and 'Mediterranean market economies' (Hall and Soskice 2001). This is not the place to go into a full-fledged analysis of different industry structures, but consider for instance the basic revenue model of newspapers. Whereas in particular newspapers in the United States have been highly dependent upon advertisement revenues (abundant from the 1970s to the 2000s, a period in which many newspapers exercised considerable monopoly power in local media markets), generating more than 80 per cent of their revenue from ads and only about 20 per cent from sales, newspapers in most European countries take in around 50 per cent of their revenue from sales, a source that is often less vulnerable to cyclical downturns. (See Figure 1.6.)

Similarly, news organisations in different countries are often embedded in very different corporate structures. Some countries (in particular smaller European ones) are dominated by a few large companies active on several platforms (like Axel Springer

Figure 1.6. Newspaper revenue from advertising and sales (2008)

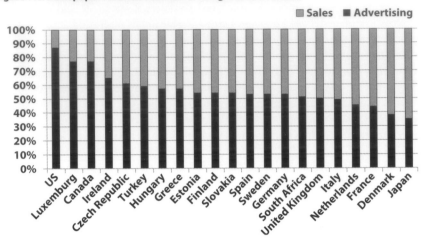

Data from OECD (2010), WAN (2009), and DDM (2008).

in Germany or the Helsingin Sanomat company in Finland). Some countries have news organisations scattered across a range of larger corporate conglomerates with diverse interests (like Dassault in France, an arms manufacturer that also owns the national newspaper *Le Figaro*). Some countries see news organisations primarily run through chains specialising in a particular medium platform (like the Gannett newspaper chain in the United States or the Trinity Mirror Group in the United Kingdom). Most see a mix of different corporate forms and kinds of ownership. These different structures have also been accompanied by variations in corporate strategy. The United States in particular has witnessed a series of mergers and acquisitions in the media sector over recent decades, often based on borrowed money and expectations of continuing high operating profits subsequently hollowed out by the recession and the increased supply of advertising space and content online and elsewhere. This has resulted in several otherwise profitable media companies finding themselves saddled with arguably unsustainable debt – in early 2010, McClatchy Company, a major newspaper chain in the United States, was spending the equivalent of 14 per cent of its revenue on interest payments alone (Liedtke 2010).

Changing journalism, changing democracy?

Faced with cyclical, technological, and longer term political, social, and economic challenges, journalism is changing today. The commercial legacy news media organisations that were the central locus of professional journalism in the twentieth century are under severe stress in some developed democracies, and undergoing an often painful transition to what may well be a diminished role in the twenty-first century. In particular in the United States and to some extent the United Kingdom, retrenchment seems likely, even as the business of journalism remains relatively stable in other countries. In France, newspapers seem to be in a more or less permanent institutionally induced crisis predating both the internet and the recession. In Finland and Germany, the sector seems robust and well-positioned to adapt to a new communication environment. In emerging democracies like Brazil and India, the industry is growing rapidly across all platforms, including print.

In addition to changes wrought by decline, stagnation, or growth in the business in individual countries, new technologies and wider societal changes are bound to change the practice of journalism, its place in the world, and its role in democracies. A range of authors have highlighted the democratic potential of some of the very same media technologies that are alleged to undermine the basis of commercial news production, stressing their potential for creating a more participatory, egalitarian, and democratic media landscape (Benkler 2006; Dutton 2009; Shirky 2008; see Hindman 2008 for a sceptical view). Irrespective of their precise implications for current and future business models, a wide range of new information and communication technologies are in the process of changing the very material character of information itself, the everyday work and practice of journalism, and its intersections with social media-wielding citizens and interlocking institutions like public relations and other professionalised communicators (Currah 2009).

In many countries, the internet is just the latest in a range of technological and organisational innovations that, in particular when coupled to widely differential levels of interest in public affairs and an abundant supply of media content, risks further fragmentation of the media landscape and exacerbates existing inequalities in people's level of political information (Turow 2006, Prior 2007). Even in countries with strong public service media organisations, this development will only be partially abated if the permanent mass audience turns out to be a thing of the past.

But even if some of the basic business challenges and technological drives of change are comparable from case to case, comparison of country cases like the ones presented in this book clearly shows that no single conclusion or firm prediction can be made about the trajectory of what remain distinct and different media systems. Comparing developments in relatively similar developed democracies can help give a more fine-grained understanding of the relative importance of cyclical, technological, and other trends in driving developments, and comparison beyond post-industrial countries – to cases like Brazil and India – only further underlines the basic point that it is premature to announce the death of the newspaper, of television, and certainly of commercial news organisations more widely.

Media observers often hold out the scenario of an 'Americanisation' or convergence upon a United States-like media system (Davis 2002; Hallin and Mancini 2004). Little in the evidence reviewed here suggests that this is a likely outcome of current developments. In fact, many American commercial legacy news organisations seem to be facing a more serious crisis than their counterparts elsewhere, and it is by no means certain that this is simply a precursor for things to come around the world. The United States may well be more of an exception and less of a forerunner than is sometimes assumed in discussions of international media developments.

We will suggest that the persistent variations and the different developments observed in media systems faced with comparable challenges imply that media managers, policy-makers, and journalists themselves face a series of choices that will together help define the future of the news. These choices are made in the context of the three kinds of cyclical, technological, and more long-term challenges outlined above and discussed in detail in the rest of the book. However, people in different countries confront them in very different settings, on the basis of very different historical legacies, and faced with very different likely outcomes. Further comparative research is clearly needed to get a better understanding of the different dynamics at play and how they intersect, and to identify more precisely what developments are of a global or nearly global character, and which ones are more regional or even national or industry-specific in character, and how they intersect and combine from country to country.

The analysis and individual case studies presented here offers a first opportunity to think through more systematically the particular combinations of change and continuity, equivalence and difference that characterise changes in the business of journalism today – and what kind of leeway this leaves for managers, journalists, policy-makers, and citizens wanting to influence these developments. We return to these issues of practical policy and to the question of the democratic implications of current changes in our concluding chapter. Let us just say here that the evidence presented in this book suggests that a one size fits all approach is not what is called for, that there are not only threats, but also plenty of opportunities ahead, and that there is still time and occasion for reinventions of and new investments in quality journalism covering public affairs and offering people the information that they need to act – not simply as consumers, but also as citizens.

References

Baker, C. Edwin (2002) *Media, Markets, and Democracy.* Cambridge: Cambridge University Press.

Benkler, Y. (2006) *The Wealth of Networks: How Social Production Transforms Markets and Freedom.* New Haven, Conn: Yale University Press.

Currah, A. (2009) *What's Happening to our News: An Investigation into the Likely Impact of the Digital Revolution on the Economics of News Publishing in the UK.* Oxford: Reuters Institute for the Study of Journalism.

Davis, A. (2002) *Public Relations Democracy: Public Relations, Politics, and the Mass Media in Britain.* Manchester: Manchester University Press.

DDM (Direction du Developpement des Medias) (2008) *La Presse écrite en 2008* (Info-MediasS #15). Paris: Direction du Developpement des Medias.

Dutton, W. H. (2009) 'The Fifth Estate Emerging through the Network of Networks', *Prometheus: Critical Studies in Innovation,* 27/1: 1.

Fernández Alonso, I., ed. (2006) *Press Subsidies in Europe.* Barcelona: Generalitat de Catalunya.

Hall, P. A., and D. W. Soskice, eds. (2001) *Varieties of Capitalism: The Institutional Foundations of Comparative Advantage.* Oxford: Oxford University Press.

Hallin, D. C., and P. Mancini (2004) *Comparing Media Systems: Three Models of Media and Politics.* Cambridge: Cambridge University Press.

Hindman, M. (2008) *The Myth of Digital Democracy.* Princeton: Princeton University Press.

Liedtke, M. (2010) 'McClatchy 2Q Earnings Plunge But Ad Slump Eases', Associated Press, 29 July.

Lund, A. B., I. Willig, and M. Blach-Ørsten (2009) *Hvor kommer nyhederne fra?, den journalistiske fødekæde i Danmark før og nu.* Århus: Ajour.

OECD (2010) *The Evolution of News and the Internet.* Paris: OECD.

Ofcom (2009) *International Communications Markets 2009.* London: Ofcom.

PricewaterhouseCoopers (2010) *Indian Media and Entertainment Outlook 2010.* Delhi: PricewaterhouseCoopers.

Prior, M. (2007) *Post-Broadcast Democracy: How Media Choice Increases Inequality in Political Involvement and Polarizes Elections*. New York: Cambridge University Press.

Pew Project for Excellence in Journalism (2010a) *How News Happens*. www.journalism. org/analysis_report/how_news_happens.

— (2010b) *The State of the News Media 2010*. New York: Journalism.org. www. stateofthenewsmedia.org/2010/.

Shirky, C. (2008) *Here Comes Everybody: The Power of Organizing Without Organizations*. London: Allen Lane.

Turow, J. (2006) *Niche Envy: Marketing Discrimination in the Digital Age*. Cambridge, Mass.: MIT Press.

WAN (2009) *World Press Trends 2009*. Paris: World Association of Newspapers.

WARC (2008) *World Advertising Trends 2008*. Henley-on-Thames: World Advertising Research Center.

— (2009) 'Top 10 Countries by Ad Expenditure, 2008': www.warc.com/LandingPages/ Data/Adspend/AdspendByCountry.asp.

Ward, D. (2003) 'State Aid or Band Aid? An Evaluation of the European Commission's Approach to Public Service Broadcasting', *Media, Culture and Society*, 25/2: 233–50.

YLE (Yleisradio Oy) (2009) *Annual Report 2009*. Helsinki: YLE.

2. A Business Perspective on Challenges Facing Journalism

Robert G. Picard

Introduction

The business of news is changing worldwide, creating economic and managerial challenges that are affecting both news organisations and how journalism is practised. The nature of the challenges is related to the life-cycle stage of news media (growth, maturation, and decline) and some global patterns are evident.

In the West, journalism is practised within well-established, mature industries that are beginning to decline in some countries. The business and practice of journalism thus face challenges associated with diminishing consumption, reduction in resources, cost cutting, consolidation, and their associated problems.

Elsewhere, journalism is in a growth stage with increasing consumption, growing resources, rising competition, and associated problems. Africa and Latin America have mixed patterns that are highly influenced by national political, social, and economic conditions. In Latin America news media are in a relatively mature stage, whereas African news media tend to be in a growth stage.

Where mature or diminishing markets exist, there is a growing sense that journalism is losing its abilities to support certain social functions. The primary challenges faced by journalism in these settings involve the organisations within which journalism takes place, the financing of the organisations and their activities, and the shifting media environment in which journalism is practised.

The concern of journalists and social observers follows a half century of news organisation growth and wealth that permitted journalists to ignore the structural and financial aspects of their industry. Indeed, as part of professionalism and unionisation, journalists gave up responsibility for business aspects to commercial or managerial interests in both commercial and non-commercial media. The result, however, was that strategic choices were often made out of concern for short-term gain rather than long-term sustainability of the news enterprise and the social needs of audiences and society.

I would like to suggest four major points for understanding the setting of journalism today: (1) news has never been a commercially viable product; (2) many observers confuse short-term problems with long-term trends; (3) shifting media use is at the heart of the contemporary financial problems of journalism; and (4) news enterprises can no longer sustain the large organisational structures and financing arrangements that were created during the age of abundant wealth

I will use some UK and US examples but the general characteristics and trends exist in many states with mature media markets, despite some variations in the dominant types of news providers, circulation and advertising revenue patterns, the degree of commercialisation of news provision, and the quality of news.

Paying for journalism

Journalists and news enterprises seem genuinely shocked by the fact that large sectors of the public are not willing to pay for news. Unfortunately, no amount of arguing that pay walls should be erected on the internet or that print prices should be raised will change that situation. The reality is that news has never been a commercially viable product and has always been funded with revenue based on its value for other things.

It is important to note that, although many in the news industry are increasingly talking about their 'business model', they in fact mean 'revenue model', which is only a small part of what comprised in a business model. Without the revenue model, of course, the enterprise collapses financially but its effectiveness is based on the value delivered through the broader business model.

Historically, the first collection and dissemination of news was funded in ancient times by emperors and kings. They used governors and officials throughout their realms to collect news and information and send it to the seat of power. The collected information was then shared with officials throughout the realm to assist in governance activities. For foreign news, the monarch sent emissaries, consuls, and ambassadors to collect news and information in places important for trade or seen as potential threats to their realms. This pattern can be seen as an imperial finance model that was designed to help manage the interests of the state.

In the Middle Ages a commercial elite financing model developed in which wealthy merchants hired correspondents in cities and states with which they traded to collect information about political and economic developments relevant to trade. Such news brought commercial advantages to the leading merchants and it was not intended for broader dissemination. It was held in confidence.

In the eighteenth and nineteenth centuries a broader social elite financing model developed to support newspapers serving the needs of the aristocracy and wider merchant classes. Even in this model, news was not profitable and newspapers were subsidised by commercial printing activities and income from other commercial activities, governments and political parties, and merchant associations.

The mass media financing model appeared in the late nineteenth and twentieth centuries, made possible by the industrial revolution, urbanisation, and the spread of wage labour. In this model news was provided for the masses at a small fee, but subsidised by advertising sales. Even in this model there is some heritage of a split press: a quality press with a heavier reliance on advertising and a tabloid or boulevard press that was still dependent on advertising but to a lesser degree than the former.

This mass media financing model remains the predominant model for financing news gathering and distribution, but its effectiveness is diminishing because news audiences are declining in mature markets. This is creating a great deal of uncertainty concerning how societies will subsidise and pay for journalism in the twenty-first century.

This question is salient because the switch between the social elite financing model and the mass media financing model was part of the democratisation of Western society, in which the greater bulk of people were brought into social decision-making and needed information and expressive opportunities in order for democratic processes to play out.

Because of the general trajectory of public policies liberalising and commercialising the media, it is now possible that we could be moving towards a system in which social elites have high-quality news and information because they can pay for it, and the bulk of the public is left with a poorer news and information delivery system. This, of course, has significant implications for democracy.

Short- and long-term developments and trends

One of the greatest challenges in considering changes in media systems and finding solutions to providing news in the future is a tendency towards short-term and narrow thought about the issues confronting us.

A good portion of the narrowness results from the tendency for media development to be seen as a zero-sum game: if television use is increasing, cinema attendance must be falling; if people are using television for news, newspaper use must be declining. In reality, audiences use a mix of media rather than any single one as a source of news, information, and entertainment.

Short-term thinking is problematic because business trends are only visible over the mid- to long-term. If one looks only at the short term, one can take contemporary developments to be a trend when they may be, in fact, an aberration. This risk is especially high in most journalists' discussions of news industry developments because they tend to operate with a relatively short-term vision because of their constant focus on current situations and immediacy in news. About the only persons with shorter term vision are news company executives, who tend to think in terms of weekly, monthly and quarterly performance.

These factors are seen in the reaction in the US to the contemporary recession and the inability of a number of newspaper firms to pay off debt. I make no argument that the 23 per cent drop in advertising during the past two years has not caused pain (see Figure 2.1), but it must be understood in a larger context. Although many commentators portray it as the death throes of the industry, it is more a result of the rapid economic downturn caused by the crises in the housing and banking industries.

In 2009 the newspaper industry in the US was a $60 billion industry (when advertising is combined with circulation income), with an average return of 12 per cent (four times better than other firms). It is not likely to disappear overnight, despite the fears of many in the industry. The contemporary financial problems destroying firms in the industry are not the result of long-term trends, but because recessions create problems for firms that have not properly managed their balance sheets. Newspapers, even those operated by the half-dozen firms that have gone bankrupt, were profitable, but not profitable enough to pay their debts. This is evidence of poor financing decisions rather than the unsustainability of the industry.

The debt problem is demonstrated by debt/equity ratios in US news organisations (total liabilities (debts) of a company compared with its equity). The New York Times

Figure 2.1. US newspaper advertising expenditures

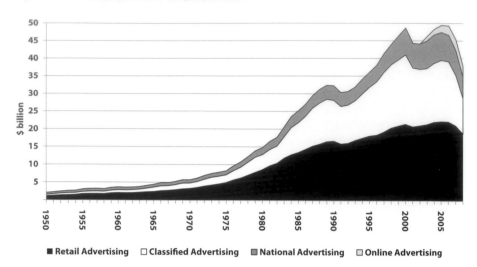

■ Retail Advertising ☐ Classified Advertising ■ National Advertising ☐ Online Advertising

Data: Newspaper Association of America

Co. has a debt/equity ratio of 5.8, the Associated Press has a ratio of 7.6, and McClatchy Newspapers scores 66.1. Normally a ratio of 1 or less is considered desirable. One can immediately see that factors other than advertising are to blame for their financial worries. The high debt ratios resulted from borrowing money to make acquisitions and to expand, something done primarily with stock swaps before the 1990s. The significant advertising growth in the 1990s, however, convinced many company boards and managers that they could pay off their debt with continuing revenue growth that ultimately did not materialise.

I do not want to give the impression that things will suddenly become rosy and return to the past, however, the current situation cannot be taken as a guide to what the challenges will be next year or the following year. The recession will pass at some point and advertising revenue will rise again, but even then revenues will continue to be affected by continuing long-term trends caused by audiences preferring other media. This means that, while it is likely that the dramatic downturn in advertising will be reversed, not all advertising will return to newspapers – especially classified and national advertising that have found benefits elsewhere – and that one cannot expect a return to the advertising revenue heyday of the 1980s and 1990s.

The real question is not whether the recession's impact is bad, but whether the industry will be sustainable after the recession, for how long, and in what form.

Problems exist in other mature markets and, like in the US, are the results of long-term trends and the condition of the current economy. In Germany, low growth rates have pushed publishers to cut costs and downsize, while simultaneously struggling to maintain their relative market positions. In France, newspapers have endured a downward trend in advertising revenue for a decade, leading to significant job cuts. In the Netherlands, layoffs and consolidation are found throughout the newspaper industry. When the economy improves, the pressure caused by the immediate situation will be relieved, but the long-term challenges will remain to be addressed.

The fickle audience

Shifting media use is the long-term trend at the heart of the contemporary business problem of news media. The fickle audience is showing itself unwilling to use news media in the numbers necessary to support the mass media finance model. We need to recognise, however, that the majority of the audience has not suddenly become uninterested in news; they were never very interested in news.

If one carefully considers media behaviour, one sees that only a small portion of the public – political, socially, and economically active members of society – is regularly interested in serious news. Anyone who has looked at patterns of circulation and viewership rapidly identifies a pattern of spikes in news use throughout the twentieth century that occurs in times of political, social, and economic crisis or disaster when news becomes salient to a larger number of people. After those crises abate, these irregular news consumers go back to their normal pattern of low news consumption.

Even before the mid-twentieth century, newspaper publishers understood that most readers were not interested in serious news, but that they read newspapers for sensational news, human interest stories, gossip, sports, entertainment, advice, and comics. These grew to contribute the majority of the content of newspapers, as well as the majority of the editorial costs, and many people read the newspapers not starting with the front section but with the sports, entertainment, and lifestyle sections.

The appearance of television, satellite television, and cable television in the second half of the twentieth century freed those less interested in news from dependence on newspapers for diversion and the lighter forms of news and information. The media emerging in the second half of the twentieth century serve entertainment and information functions better for those relatively uninterested in news and they have been shifting their use from newspapers to those other media and watching entertainment rather than news broadcasts when they have the opportunity to do so. This growth in the breadth of media is illustrated with examples from the UK in Figure 2.2.

Although newspapers were present throughout the twentieth century, the number of media increased in terms of breadth and they have expanded tremendously in terms of depth (more radio and television stations, more websites, etc.). These have increased choices for consumers. They can go many places for news, information, public affairs

Figure 2.2. Timeline of appearance of newer media in the United Kingdom

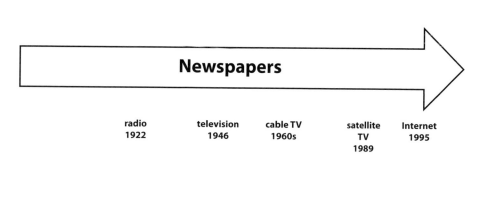

and entertainment. With more choice, the inevitable result is smaller audiences and reduced revenue for media companies. This issue is shown by the trend of US newspaper consumption over the past century (Figure 2.3).

Figure 2.3. US newspaper circulation per 1,000 population

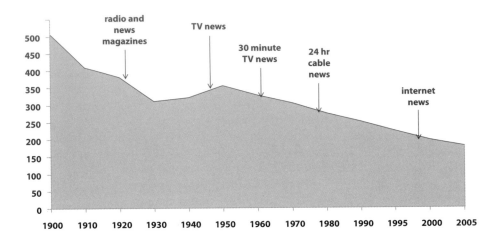

Data: Newspaper Association of America and the author

Some have erroneously blamed the internet for the problems of journalism, but the trend in newspaper consumption has not changed significantly since the arrival of internet news. The internet has not caused the problem for newspapers; though it compounds it.

Those who believe newspapers can shift operations online and easily monetise news on the internet seem to forget the competition of free news that is provided by a range of media, including some that provide high-quality content: public service radio and television, commercial radio and television, internet portals (many of whom buy news services from major news agencies), and free newspapers.

Challenges of news organisations

The fundamental challenges facing news enterprises today are that they can no longer sustain the large organisational structures and financing arrangements created during the age of abundant wealth. The diminishing audience and lack of growth in or diminishing advertising expenditures make it impossible to continue to maintain the scope and scale of operations.

The second half of the twentieth century, particularly its last 25 years, were incredibly profitable for media firms and they used the financial resources to grow, to create large – often global – organisations with heavy overheads and financing costs. Between 1950 and 2000, advertising income for newspapers nearly tripled in real terms, making newspaper firms extraordinarily wealthy. Newspaper companies became publicly traded firms, acquired other newspapers and other media firms, built fine facilities, increased their number of personnel, and bought corporate jets. Money was plentiful, journalists were relatively well compensated with wages and benefits, and resources existed for many of the kinds of reporting that journalists cherish. This growth can be illustrated by News Corp., which had revenues of $6.7 billion in 1990 ($10.9 billion today adjusted for inflation). Last year, the company had revenues of $30.4 billion.

Even not-for-profit firms benefited as the economy grew, obtaining more financial resources from their funders and engaging in a wide range of commercial activities that brought in even more funds. The BBC, for example, had an income of £220 million in 1975 (£1.7 billion today when adjusted for inflation). In 2009 its income was £4.605 billion, 2.7 times more money in real terms than it had in 1975. It used the money to increase the size of its operations, the number of channels it provided, to create multiple facilities throughout the UK and the world, and to expand into many other kinds of media operations.

Large enterprises have grown through start-ups and acquisitions that have diversified their operations into a wide range of media activities and have increased the number of titles, channels, and sites they operate. Although this has brought growth to company revenues, the average audiences for their media operations have become smaller because many other firms have entered the print, television, and internet markets and fragmented the audience. The largest media conglomerates today typically serve audiences that are 30 to 60 per cent smaller than they were a quarter a century ago. The side effects of such growth are that size creates complexity, engenders inefficiency, and makes adjusting to new realities difficult. The current size of many news organisations is a source of many industry challenges today. The growth of advertising has not only ended, but consumer expenditures for news media are declining and public willingness to pay for public service broadcasting has waned. The resources that have made both large public and commercial news operations possible are being stripped from the industries, leaving them unable to pay the huge costs created by their extraordinary growth during the financial golden age.

So where do we go from here?

We are now confronted with the very real questions of how we finance and organise journalism in the twenty-first century. I want to suggest that we should not focus on how we can save particular enterprises but rather the underlying functions of news gathering and providing the public access to news and information. These functions are what are important to society; not the specific forms or organisations in which they are pursued.

From the business perspective it is clear that we will need smaller more agile organisations in the future. They will have to take more entrepreneurial approaches to creating the financial resources available for their operations and be more innovative in terms of the news products and services they provide. In the past, news organisations have typically tried to be stand-alone organisations, but in the digital world they will need to rely more on alliances, networking, and cooperation than in the past.

Underlying all of this must be a rethinking of the entire business model of media and how it creates value for customers, for itself and for society. Newspapers (whether in print, online, or e-readers) will have to focus their efforts on providing news and information not available elsewhere, in a better form than on the other platforms, and of better quality. Doing the same things in the same old ways will not work in the future.

It is likely, too, we will see a split in news provision. Elite providers of higher quality news and information with a higher price will coexist with low-cost or free providers of quick and easy news, plus significant amounts of sports, entertainment, and lifestyle information. In many cases, these providers will belong to the same print, internet, or broadcasting company.

To finance these activities news enterprises will change and require engagement in a variety of new organisational activities. Income will increasingly come from multiple sources – consumers, advertisers, syndication, income from events and unrelated commercial activities, and trusts and donations. The latter, of course, may require new thinking in tax and charities laws.

As we address how to create a sustainable future for news, and how we can reasonably transform the industry to achieve it, we must focus not on the past but on a vision of the future and how to achieve it. We must focus on what democracy needs, not on what current new enterprises or journalists need. We must focus on how to inform those who are engaged and how to engage those who are not. We must focus on not merely national needs, but regional and local news and information needs as well.

This requires that we firmly root our efforts in the fundamental values of education, citizenship, and democracy. While we must be pragmatic about the business of news, we must not lose sight of the righteous work in which we are engaged.

3. Online News: Recent Developments, New Business Models and Future Prospects

Sacha Wunsch Vincent

Introduction

This chapter provides an overview of recent developments in the provision, consumption, and dissemination of online news, business issues raised by the changing online news ecosystem, and future prospects for journalism in an online news environment. It is based on the OECD (2010) report *The Evolution of News and the Internet*, which provides a more comprehensive survey of the news industry in a range of developed democracies.

Technology has acted as a strong driver of online news and the gathering of information online to make meaningful decisions affecting private and public life. In terms of platforms and networks, the increased broadband availability at cheaper prices has boosted online activities such as online news consumption. News distribution over the internet increasingly relies on new information distribution technologies such as news aggregation and syndication technologies (RSS technologies), blogs and services such as Google News (OECD 2006). The way users today skim stories, shift to other pages, return or not, has profound implications for which types of information get wide readership and how news is consumed and digested, and this has important implications for how news is produced to attract the readers' attention. In terms of news production, online news sites rely on sophisticated database and visual technologies to narrate a story and to make data and facts accessible online in a manner which was unheard of recently. Instead of being pure internet pages displaying information, such as in typical offline newspapers, they will be interactive, multimedia databases which can pool and mix different archives, search and interact with the document database. In terms of reception, rapid advances in mobile technologies, wireless networks and user interfaces have enabled mobile news delivery. In particular, the introduction of smartphones and the release of e-readers have started to change how people are accessing information. E-readers, such as the recently launched iPad, are also expected to provide a new opportunity for pay per view or online subscription news.

Developments in news consumption

The internet is now a critical source for information and news. 'Reading news online' is a favourite and increasingly important internet activity (Figure 3.1). In terms of frequency of internet activity it scores just below the most popular internet activities: emailing and searching for information about goods and services. In some OECD countries, more than half of the population is using the internet to read newspapers online (up to 77 per cent in Korea) but at the minimum 20 per cent of the population is doing so. Social drivers of online news are the desire for constant updates on the go matching the greater mobility of users, the desire for personalised information and to be able to access multiple pages on the same topic or from different geographic origins, to participate in the creation of content online and to 'witness' and share news (OECD 2006).

Reliable data on the relative importance of online news versus other more traditional forms of news are not widely available. In many countries, TV and newspapers are still the most important sources of news but this is shifting, with newspapers losing ground more quickly to the internet than TV. In countries with advanced mobile broadband solutions such as Korea, offline newspaper reading is already less popular today (51.5 per cent of population) than online newspaper reading (77.3 per cent) according to surveys. In the United States, the internet has become an important source for news (40 per cent of all Americans went online in 2008 to gather news), just ahead of print newspapers (35 per cent), but behind television (70 per cent) (Pew 2006). For the most part, reading news online complements other forms of news rather than displacing it.

In general, younger age groups are much more active online news readers (Figure 3.2). However, according to official statistics, it is not the youngest age brackets (16–24 years) which are most active but slightly older groups – usually 25-34 year-olds for most OECD countries, but in some countries with a strong record on broadband such as Norway the 35–44 or 45–54 year age groups score high as they too have become used to relying on the internet for the past decade. Avid online news readers are likely to be professionals and also readers of printed news.

Furthermore, most surveys show that active offline newspaper readers tend to read more news online (Comscore 2008). Fewer and fewer persons rely on printed news alone. Surveys in France, Germany and in other countries show that offline readers actually are increasingly complementing their readership through online news. Still only very few people rely exclusively on online news. Countries with advanced mobile broadband solutions such as Korea, where offline newspaper reading is less popular than online newspaper reading, are the exception. Well-informed news readers will tend to supplement their news consumption online.

Despite these findings, the share of people who read only online news is likely to grow rapidly with new generations who start using the internet early in life. The real concern however is the fact that a significant portion of young people are not reading news at all or only irregularly. In France, only 10 per cent of 18–24 year olds read a daily newspaper, about half as compared to a decade ago. In the United States the share of 18 to 24 year olds who got no news at all the previous day has risen from 25 per cent to 34 per cent in the past ten years (Pew Internet Survey). This finding is most alarming and would need more longitudinal studies to assess whether eventually these younger age groups pick up news readership of some form at an older age. Also data for some OECD countries indicate that heavy internet use does not translate into heavy use of online news for younger age brackets (ACMA 2008). All reports in OECD countries confirm that internet users report a large increase in time spent reading

Figure 3.1. Proportion of individuals reading/downloading online newspapers/news magazines over the internet for private purposes (% of individuals aged 16–74)

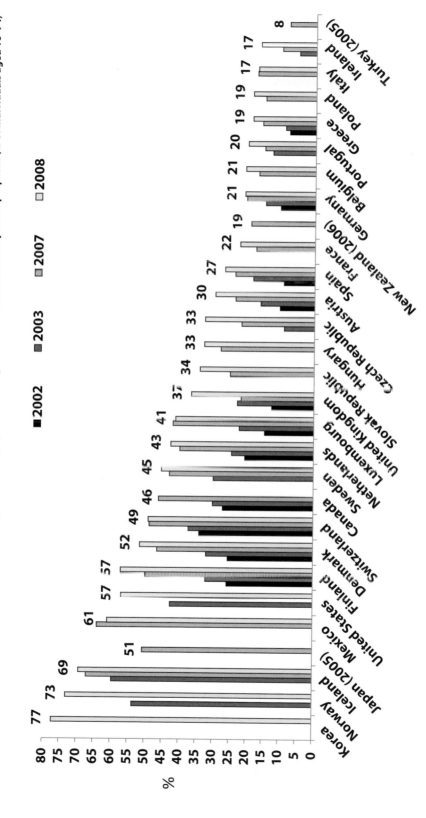

■ 2002   ■ 2003   ■ 2007   □ 2008

Data from OECD (2010), based on OECD ICT database, Korea, Korea, Japan and New Cronos, Eurostat. Latest official data from the US broadband survey is from 2003. The 2003 value is taken from Pew Internet. Figures indicated in graph are rounded.

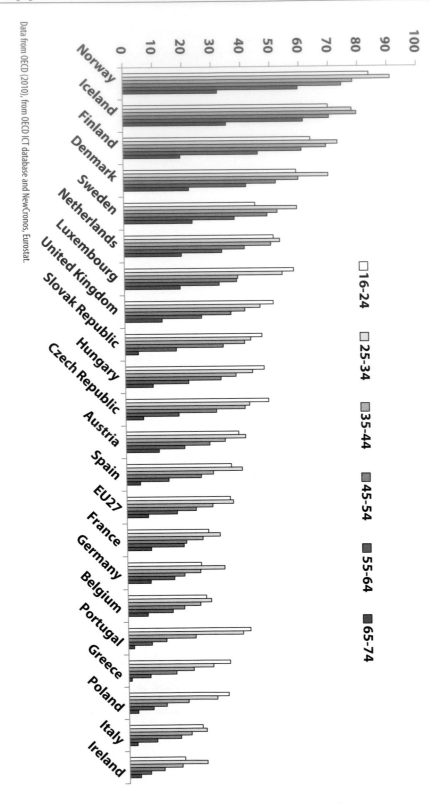

Figure 3.2. Individuals who used the internet in the last three months for reading/ downloading online newspaper/news-magazine by age (% of total population, 2008)

Data from OECD (2010), from OECD ICT database and NewCronos, Eurostat.

online newspapers (i.e. sites of newspapers), but, for most people, online readership is more *ad hoc*, irregular, and sporadic than print newspaper readership used to be.

One general problem with readership surveys is that one rarely finds out about the frequency, intensity, and depth of news readership – offline versus online in particular (minutes spent reading offline news vs. minutes spent reading online news, thoroughness and breadth of readership online vs. offline). Surveys of print newspapers show that on average OECD readers spent about 20–30 minutes reading a daily newspaper (WAN 2003–9). The time spent reading print newspapers is still enormous and unlikely to be challenged by current online news readership. Crude estimates suggest that about 92 per cent of newspaper reading is done in print and 8 per cent takes place online (Progressive Review 2009). However, these values apply to a declining print readership, they might vary a lot between users and they are hard to compare directly to internet news readership which mostly relies on metrics such as counting online page views (page impressions per unique visitor) for online newspaper sites, while largely ignoring all other forms of online news consumption such as news aggregators, pure players or mobile news.

Online news readers get a variety of news from different sources, i.e. just in time news alerts over their mobile phone, via various online news sources at work, and while surfing the internet in the evening. Their internet access to news is increasingly daily and for those working in offices or owning a Smartphone the access to news can be continual throughout the day, rather than just in the morning. Online news readers come to the news via search engines, via email newsletters or mail forwards, or via aggregation tools. Sometimes they spend only a few seconds or minutes on a particular article (or headline, video or picture) before they leave that particular news site to find similar articles elsewhere. Some sites have very high audience retention and loyalty (Spiegel online in Germany, Liberation in France, BBC in the United Kingdom, etc.). But overall the retention of readers for any one single news source online is likely to be low, compared to offline newspapers. In terms of capturing the whole news spectrum rather than focusing on individual stories, some online readers might never get an overview of all news through the home page of a particular news site in this way. Others however will use news aggregators, newspaper home pages or the email or mobile phone service of online news sites to get such overviews. In any case, this more fragmented way of reading the news allows them to mix different sources (including different media formats) and compile their own personalised information. It will be very hard to turn back the clock on these new media consumption habits.

Internet traffic to online news sites

In all OECD countries, the internet traffic to online news sites has grown over recent years. Available Experian Hitwise data for the United Kingdom, the United States, Canada and Australia show that about 5 per cent of all internet visits are related to visiting sites dedicated exclusively to online news. This includes visits to sites such as newspaper internet sites but also other news sources such as news aggregators, internet sites of news broadcasters, news services of search engines, etc. It excludes the main home page of internet portals or other internet intermediaries which often have some news on their site but which on this particular page are not predominantly focused on news (and thus are not classified as online news sites in these internet usage statistics). It also excludes the use of news via email, SMS or on mobile phones, social networking tools such as MySpace or Twitter and many blogs which are increasingly popular for the diffusion of news online. So in total a much higher share of internet visits can be associated with some news consumption.

More recently newspaper websites have seen strong growth in their own pages, with several million unique users per month in most OECD countries. Again the main driver of this trend is a strong increase in referrals by Google, search engines and increasingly also social networks. Related other reasons are better search engine optimisation and the more effective use of paid search. Most surveys which test for the willingness to pay for online news find that it is very low but increasing. There are exceptions such as the *Wall Street Journal* which has very effectively been able to charge for online news. According to PricewaterhouseCoopers, some surveys show an increasing customer acceptance of paid content, in particular for online newspapers (see Editorsweblog 2009). However, it remains to be seen if the expressed intentions of those surveyed translate into actual payments.

In contrast, print newspaper readership has always been almost exclusively national. Intermediaries such as Google or Yahoo! News do not capture a large share of the news-related traffic. News aggregators make up less than 10 per cent of total news-related traffic in the United States and more like 5 per cent in the United Kingdom and Australia. Still, news aggregators such as Digg, StumbleUpon, NetVibes which started as rather small tools constantly increase their market shares. Moreover, pure players (online-only news providers) are growing in importance fast, with about 25 per cent of all news-related visits in the United States. In some markets for which we have data the access to foreign news sites is an important component of the online news landscape. In particular, English-speaking sites draw significant traffic from abroad.

There are considerable national variations in online news traffic. In the United Kingdom, the BBC dominates online news, with much larger shares of traffic than Sky News and Yahoo (Figure 3.3). Online newspaper internet sites also receive a fair share of individual traffic (*Daily Mail*, *Telegraph*, etc.), but at a lower level than the BBC site. Sites such as MSN or other news aggregators do not receive more traffic than well-known newspaper sites and are also overtaken by online-only news sites (Figure 3.3). In the United States, in contrast, print organisations capture most

Figure 3.3. Visits by type of news and media provider in % of the total internet visits to the online news category (Aug. 2009)

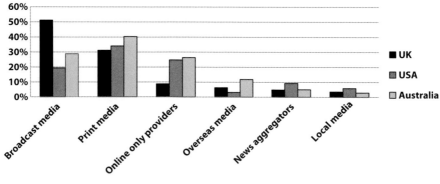

Data: Experian Hitwise for the OECD (2010).

traffic, followed by broadcasters (MSNBC, CNN), and by online-only providers, and only then comes news aggregators such as Yahoo! News (Figure 3.3). Australia lies somewhere inbetween the US and the UK experience. In Korea and most likely also in Japan, internet portals dominate online news visits. While search engines and others may play a lesser role in actually disseminating news, they are crucial for spurring traffic to online news sites, followed by email and social networks (Figure 3.4). Figures for the UK show that 25–35 per cent of traffic to news websites comes from one single prominent search engine alone.

Figure 3.4. Upstream sources of online news traffic (% of total upstream traffic sent to news categories, Aug. 2009)

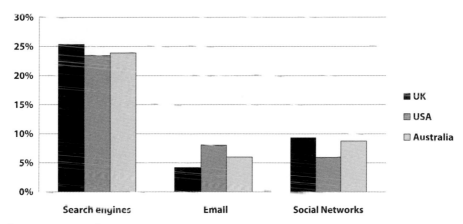

Data: Experian Hitwise for the OECD (2010).

A changing news ecosystem

Due to the rise of new technologies and the internet in particular, a novel news ecosystem has emerged which is significantly different from the traditional model. Changing consumption patterns mean new and modified business models for all media actors, including for example the written press. Technological advances, particularly digitalisation and the internet, are driving convergence and a form of news distribution which crosses traditional sectoral and geographic boundaries. A consequence of these changes is that information providers with very different histories (TV, newspapers, internet companies, etc.) find themselves competing head-to-head in a new, very complex and multifaceted online news environment which is inherently global in nature. New actors emerge which challenge the role of gatekeepers and shift power to new intermediaries. While cross-border sales of printed newspapers have always been rather marginal, online news consumption is becoming more and more international.

In this environment, news organisations have to focus on cross-media publishing across various platforms, with changes to the content production and distribution process. The immediacy of the internet means that many newspaper websites need to update news more often than their own editorial staff can handle, as well as needing multimedia content such as photos, audio and video feeds. And in the internet context business models often have to be rethought as charging for bundles of news content (as when buying a full physical newspaper) is often not a functioning online business practice.

Figure 3.5. A stylised online news value network

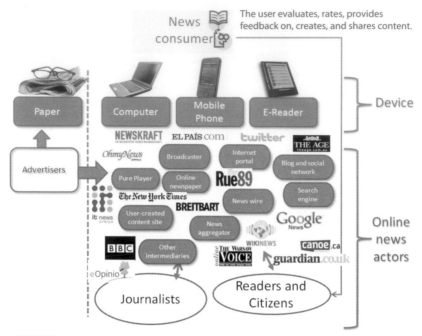

From OECD (2010).

Figure 3.5 presents a stylised online news value chain which entails an increased role of users as contributors to news, a large number of online news actors and intermediaries (and connections between them) and finally a number of new distribution modes and technologies to consume news (e.g. a laptop). In this new context, the production and dissemination of news is a much more interactive and multi-directional, rather than linear process – a value network rather than a value chain, if you will. News wire agencies, newspapers and news broadcasters remain an important source of news and information for other actors in the value chain (including bloggers, etc.) which feed from them to adapt and comment on the news. But traditional actors also share and feed from each other (for instance, a newspaper picking up on a story floated by an online-only newspaper or the internet site of a broadcaster following up on a scandal raised by a blogger). A constant updating of news is taking place, with journalists and other news contributors monitoring, distilling, and repackaging an ever-increasing amount of information. In this online news ecosystem, users also increasingly become diffusers, commentators, and creators of news.

While, before the internet, traditional news organisations were largely in charge of the content creation, their form, their diffusion and relevant pricing, this has now changed radically. Similarly to other digital content value chains on the internet, established actors have to rethink their position and way of generating revenues in a complex new ecosystem alongside these other internet actors. Some of these online news actors such as certain search engines or internet portals are very dominant when it comes to their share of overall internet traffic and thus access to the news consumer.

Many of these other actors which in part disintermediate newspapers will not necessarily be interested in generating money by selling news content as newspapers do.

Most actually hope to rely on online advertising alone to generate sufficient revenues. Others will sell other services. Some will just piggyback on information provided by newspaper organisations to attract traffic and advertising to their site and offer it to their users as one of many other useful and often free services. However, a new trend is also that online-only businesses such as AOL increasingly hire journalists themselves. All of these new online actors have in common that they do not share the large fixed-cost base which traditional news organisations do to provide in-depth and varied reporting and to operate physical manufacturing, distribution, and administration.

Today the device or network service providers which did not play any role in the traditional model suddenly also control the access to the end consumer and have a large degree of bargaining power with content providers. Similarly to other new digital content set-ups (e.g. Apple in the case of music, Amazon in the case of e-books), news organisations have to enter into strategic relationships and revenue-sharing models with a new set of important actors.

Changed online news business models

On the internet, digital content business models are emerging, some of which mirror offline models (pay-per-item sales or subscriptions, for example) and some of which are new. Digital content industries are still mainly experimenting with how to generate revenues online, but the seven main and existing generic categories can be summarised as follows (see OECD 2008):

(1) voluntary donations and contributions;
(2) digital content sales (pay-per-track, pay-per-view, pay-per-game, etc.);
(3) subscription-based revenues;
(4) advertising-based revenues;
(5) selling goods and services (including virtual items) to the audience;
(6) selling user data and customised market research;
(7) licensing content and technology to other providers.

In the case of news, direct revenues generated online from news consumers are still rather small. Most if not all revenues by all above-mentioned actors are generated via online advertising or online classified ads (revenue model 4 above) and potentially content licensing. The heavy reliance on online advertising as a source of revenue applies both to news organisations as well as to bloggers, profit or non-profit online-only news sites (pure players), internet portals, search engines, and others. More recently, new initiatives were launched via internet actors to increase the traffic to newspaper organisations' websites and thereby increase their advertising revenues (e.g. Google FastFlip). Personal data of users make it possible to sell more lucrative targeted advertising. A number of other internet actors (search engines, etc.) are using news to retain attention at their sites and to provide interesting content to their customer base. However, their revenues are also generated either via advertising or by selling unrelated services (professional mail accounts, etc.).

Newspapers and in particular also news wires have also licensed their content to third parties and started collecting revenues by this means (e.g. the use of Associated Press headlines and full articles by Google or the use of headlines and full news items by Korean internet portals). In this set-up many news-related organisations in the

Table 3.1. Online news actors, impacts and strategies

Journalists

The development of digital content has had a major impact on journalists' working lives and on the way in which they work. Journalists working within a traditional newspaper organisation now have to cater to both offline and online audiences at the same time (potentially also being responsible for video, blogs, etc.). This might lead to an increased work load, the need for new (multimedia) skills and greater openness to reader feedback or also citizen journalism.

Journalists will feel the increased pressure on budgets and may face potential layoffs (the same applies in particular to freelance journalists and photographers who now compete with free resources). Few journalists will be able to increase their revenues due to their increased recognition. Some journalists may – voluntarily or involuntarily – create online news ventures or start working outside the traditional news industry. Some of the online-only news experiments and blogs are often effectively funded by redundancy packages of journalists who were formerly employed by traditional news organizations.

Newspapers

Most newspapers have set up online presences which employ new technologies to push out and distribute information As part of a multiplatform strategy, newspapers are developing into a 24-hour, local news-gathering media company which distributes news among our different platforms: print, online and mobile.

Newspapers are experimenting with new models with some having trialled a pay-per-read walled garden (e.g. Times Select) models. These for the most part did not work. A few others have had more success (Wall Street Journal). 2010 will mark the time where newspapers will try – one more time – to restrict access and raise money by selling content. The search of newspapers for profitable business models and new relationships with other news and internet actors is far from concluded.

News wire agencies

Some news agencies continue to be wholesalers of news to newspapers, broadcasters and websites and others who distribute the news to the end consumer. News agencies benefit from an increased number of online sites which rely on news but which do not have the resources to produce it.

But there is also a general trend for agencies to provide direct-to-consumer services (mostly on their advertising-financed sites but also increasingly on mobile platforms) and specialised, targeted premium information rather than supplying to other intermediaries (such as newspapers) and in fact disintermediating them. At the same time, other news actors are increasingly hesitant to pay large wire agency fees, sometimes cancelling their subscriptions and relying on cheaper or free news material. Broadcasters such as CNN are planning to set up their own news agencies.

Broadcasters (including public broadcasters and 24-hour TV news providers)

All major news broadcasters now have an online presence – ranging from small video teasers and text news to more sophisticated offerings with video podcasts; either special online videos or delayed reposting of news editions which were displayed 'on the air' hours earlier, extensive news clips, and on-demand archived content.

These are mostly financed by advertising and by – still to a minor degree – the sale of on-demand content. In large media conglomerates other forms of content (entertainment, etc.) are cross-subsidising the news department. Public sector broadcasters continue to be financed by taxpayer money (and sometimes advertising).

Pure online news players

Recent years have also seen the emergence of pure online news entities which are intensive in their use of news distribution technologies such as video blogs. The sites often specialise in certain news niches and some sites are exclusively focused on citizen journalism. Their role as gatekeepers to the end customer is growing.

These are driven by new technologies, seed money, citizen journalism and journalists who have voluntarily or involuntarily left traditional news entities. Some of these are for profit whereas others are non-profits (supported by philanthropic funding, for example). Few for-profit entities have yet to generate enough revenues to be self-sustaining.

Internet portals and search infomediaries

Increasingly, new syndication models are emerging in which internet portals or other infomediaries act as online news aggregators – sometimes in partnership and revenue sharing agreements with news creators and sometimes without. News aggregators mostly rely and depend on content produced by others, originating from wire agencies, photographers, newspapers et al. However, a new trend is also that these businesses increasingly hire journalists themselves. The sites are mostly financed by advertising or selling services unrelated to news. News is used to further cultivate a 'captive audience' and internet traffic.

News platform providers (smartphones, e-readers, e-commerce merchants)

New technology platform providers are emerging around e-readers and Smartphones. This is either driven by intermediaries which repurpose news services for certain new platforms (e.g. the iPhone), network providers or by the hardware producers themselves. In the latter cases, gatekeepers to the end-customer will ask for a cut of the revenues from news providers.

value chain have entered into content-sharing or licensing agreements (e.g. the *New York Times* showing TechCrunch articles, a tech blog, or Le Monde.com affording full access to *El País*). The financial rewards generated through these licensing deals are mostly undisclosed.

Newspapers and other news organisations have experimented with trying to sell access to news on a pay-per-item basis or via subscriptions (revenue models 2 and 3 above) but – for the most part – revenues are still negligible (in particular those coming from a pay-per-item basis). There are notable exceptions such as the *Wall Street Journal* and the *Financial Times*, but the first wave of trials of paid news in the first half of this decade has mostly been a failure, with readers turning away from the respective site and accessing news for free elsewhere. In 2010, newspapers were gearing up for a second trial to charge for online news content. Table 3.1 summarises the approaches and business models for the different online news actors.

Future prospects: opportunities and challenges in a novel online news ecosystem

Some observers note that news production and distribution have never been more dynamic and independent than today. In this view, the internet enables greater access to a more varied source of news. Eventually the nature and speed of the technology and increased participation help to uncover the truth in a much more efficient way than in previous environments, and innovative forms of journalism build novel bridges to readers. The end of newspapers would not mean the end of news gathering and diffusion. In fact, in this view, the current online news ecosystem ends a period in which news monopolies controlled the news and access to it.

- *The internet as major source of information and diversity*: The internet offers the ability to access information sources, including in countries with less media freedom or with less access to a well-funded, impartial press. Furthermore, the internet and related technologies offer greater access to information for journalists and citizens, making it more difficult to cover up corruption or other secrets.[1]

- *New sources of entrepreneurial and non-market news organisations*: Next to citizen journalists, the internet has led to a rise of web publishers and entrepreneurial journalists with for-profit and not-for-profit ventures which might more than compensate for the reduction in traditional news outlets.

- *The appeal of new multiple sources of information*: Proponents of this view argue that the credibility and quality of the traditional news media were actually at stake long before the rise of the internet. The high concentration of media ownership (and government control of the media in some countries), the ever-greater importance of advertisers, the proximity between journalists and the people they cover, the

---

[1] See 'Press Freedom and the Internet', *The Economist* (17 Oct. 2009) showing how the internet and bloggers in particular make censored material available when traditional media are bound by law to refrain from publishing or reporting information.

increasing influence of public relations (PR) agencies, further cuts in the quality and diversity of editorial content, and other challenges raised below have reduced their credibility, further decreasing the trust and interest of readers (as demonstrated by survey data).

Other observers, however, deplore that the 'golden age' of newspapers and journalism when quality and reliability were arguably higher is now sadly gone. They maintain that the growing financial pressures and the emergence of 'free news' put this golden age increasingly at stake. According to this view, the economic foundations of modern journalism are crumbling and there are few alternative models in sight which would guarantee satisfactory news coverage. The accuracy, quality and diversity of news are at risk, and the economic downturn has intensified this trend.

The list of challenges posed to the contemporary news system is long and often an amalgam of rather distinct items which are often not a direct consequence of novel forms of news distribution alone.

- *Growing resource and time pressure leading to sparser and lower quality coverage ('churnalism')*: In practical terms, the growing lack of resources and the necessity to update news around the clock in a 24-hour newsroom have resulted in the reduction of bureaux, layoffs and a consequent reduction of in-house editorial content and potentially quality and increased reliance on cheaper and softer news with entertainment value and appeal to advertisers.

- *Greater homogeneity of news*: It is argued that time and financial pressure have led to a greater reliance on outside news sources (mostly the wire services but also arguably partial press release material, news agency feeds, blogging and non-journalistic sources, including readers) rather than the publisher's own editorial content (Australian Press Council 2008; Currah 2009).

- *Excessive commenting?*: To differentiate themselves, offline and online news journalists have an increased tendency to comment and opine rather than report the news. The rise of personalised blogs, columns with the photograph of a journalist and other such developments foster this trend of 'star commentators' (Currah 2009).

- *Increased fragmentation*: The internet fragments audiences to an even greater extent than other media and may lead to increased differences in levels of political information amongst citizens.

- *High-quality news increasingly restricted to an elite?*: In this general context of faltering quality of the news, a few news outlets might opt for the production of high-quality news which might however be restricted to a small number of persons that can afford to pay for it (Poulet 2009).

As usual the truth is likely to lie somewhere in the middle. In fact, given the very dynamic state of affairs with respect to new technologies, new business models, and new actors on the scene, the exact impacts and outcomes are hard to predict. In general, it is important not to infer that the internet or novel online news actors are the cause of all of the challenges faced by the traditional news system.

The past has also shown that established media often resist new technology platforms much better than one would expect, and that often very complementary relationships can emerge. Nonetheless, it will be of critical importance to understand how news gathering and content creation will be impacted over the next months and years. Currently, one can be concerned about whether the supply of high-quality journalism is secure. The prerogative of policy-makers should be to secure independent news production, regardless of through which medium – paper or not – this objective is attained.

References

Australian Communications and Media Authority (ACMA) (2008) *Telecommunications Today – Report 6: Internet Activity and Content*; www.acma.gov.au/WEB/STANDARD/pc=PC_9058>

Australian Press Council (2008) *State of the News Print Media in Australia*. Sydney: Australian Press Council; www.presscouncil.org.au/pcsite/activities/guides/gpr284.html

Comscore (2008) 'Younger, Heavy Online News Consumers are Not Newspaper Readers'; http://ir.comscore.com/releasedetail.cfm?releaseid=299286

Currah, A. (2009) *What's Happening to our News?* Oxford: Reuters Institute for the Study of Journalism.

Editorsweblog (2009) 'PwC: Consumers Willing to Pay for Online News'; www.editorsweblog.org/world_newspaper_congress/2009/12/pwc_consumers_willing_to_pay_for_online.php

OECD (2006) *OECD Information Technology Outlook 2006*. Paris: OECD.

— (2008) *OECD Information Technology Outlook 2008*. Paris: OECD.

— (2010) *The Evolution of News and the Internet*. Paris: OECD.

Pew (2006) Online News: For Many Home Broadband Users, the Internet is a Primary News Source, 22 March, PEW Internet and American Life project.

Poulet, B. (2009) *La Fin des journaux et l'avenir de l'information*. Paris: Éditions Gallimard.

Progressive Review (2009) 'Study: Only 3% of Newspaper Reading is Online'; http://prorev.com/2009/08/study-only-3-of-newspaper-reading-is.html

WAN (2003–9) *World Press Trends*. Annual reports and online database (and data supplied directly by World Association of Newspapers).

4. The Strategic Crisis of German Newspapers

Frank Esser and Michael Brüggemann

Introduction

This chapter argues that, in spite of the economic crisis that has affected the media in Germany, the infrastructure of the German media system is still suited to providing for accountability journalism as a core element of the democratic constitution of society. The conditions for journalism are still more favourable than in some other Western countries, due to stable market structures, policy provisions for public service broadcasting and a media culture heavily influenced by the idea of a public sphere as a critical forum for debate about issues of common concern. There are, however, pressures that will likely aggravate in the long run if left unresponded to. This chapter identifies five countermeasures pursued by German media organisations to tackle the challenges of declining revenues from traditional advertising, shifting audience preferences, and the internet. As a complementary strategy, German publishers have drawn up a wish list of media policy responses designed to improve general framework conditions of the press, and they lobby very hard in Berlin and Brussels for their implementation at the national and European level. Assessing the overall scope of the current difficulties, the chapter concludes that we are observing a 'strategic crisis of newspaper publishers' but no general media crisis, and certainly no crisis of democracy in Germany.

The infrastructures of accountability journalism

Germany's media market is one of the biggest in the world in terms of newspaper circulation, advertising budgets, number of journalists, and number of news outlets. The market composition has been remarkably stable in recent decades. The *infrastructure* discussed below is part of a broader *culture* of public communication that is influenced by the concept of 'Öffentlichkeit' (public sphere) as elaborated most prominently in the works of Jürgen Habermas and rooted in the idea of self-government guided by the free and rational public deliberation of citizens. This culture of public communication is articulated in broadcasting regulation with emphasis on the idea of public service rather than pure entertainment, a sound professional culture of journalism with a focus on analysis and exchange of opinions, and a well-established culture of newspaper reading. Three pillars provide for the relatively stable infrastructure of accountability journalism in Germany.

1. Following the model of the BBC, a *strong public broadcasting* structure was established after the Second World War and regulations were introduced that also oblige private channels to include a minimum level of journalism in their news programming. The public broadcasting scene is very rich: Germany is one of the few countries in the world with two rival nation-wide public TV groups (ARD, ZDF) which compete not only with private channels but also with one another. Public broadcasting was installed to provide the 'Grundversorgung', i.e. to cover all basic audience needs with regard to information, education, and entertainment as defined by German media law. In addition to this wide range of public service channels, there is a multitude of commercial TV stations with two big chains, RTL group and Sat.1/ProSieben group, as the main players. Table 4.1 shows that the average time spent watching different TV channels and their market share remained remarkably stable over the last decade.

2. The second pillar of stability is made up of the *well-established publishing houses* that dominate the print media market in Germany, some of which have become big players in the global publishing market. The top three publishing houses are Bertelsmann with a turnover of €18.8 billion, Springer (€2.6 billion), and Holtzbrinck (€2.5 billion) (figures from 2007 as reported by Dreier 2009: 258). Only Springer AG is listed on the stockmarket (since 1985) but half of its shares are in family hands. Holtzbrinck is still owned by the different heirs of the founder of the company; Bertelsmann is partly in family hands and partly owned by its own foundation (Bertelsmann Stiftung). Publishers like Axel Springer pursued at the same time political and economic missions. Therefore, in spite of not being profitable for many years the conservative quality newspaper *Die Welt* was subsidised by Springer with the profits from other businesses of the publishing house, in particular the tabloid *Bild* (which sells more than three million copies every day, making it the world's fifth biggest daily newspaper: WAN 2009). This culture of publishing to contribute to public discourse has been giving way to a more commercial logic. This change is linked to the heirs of the newspaper founders taking over the business from the founders who mostly started the newspapers shortly after the end of the Second World War.

3. The economic strength of the publishing houses is grounded in a deep-rooted *division of the market along regional and editorial lines* which provides for monopoly dividends in the respective markets. The regional press occupies three-quarters of the daily newspaper market, and even the national newspapers have a strong regional base (e.g. the *Süddeutsche Zeitung* based in Munich and *Frankfurter Allgemeine Zeitung* based in Frankfurt both draw a large chunk of their readership from their

respective area). The German press market had already consolidated in the 1960s and 1970s. It resulted in five large publishing companies that control 45 per cent of the daily newspaper market share (Röper 2008). The remaining market share is in the hands of medium-sized companies which are often run by families and could count on profits well above a 10 per cent return on investment thanks to their local monopolies. Furthermore, the national broadsheet market is divided along ideological lines. With historical roots in the party press, newspapers still can be clearly classified as being more or less liberal or conservative. Regional roots and political orientations go hand in hand with a strong reader loyalty: readers subscribe to their newspaper rather than buying it at the newsstand and they are even willing to pay higher prices for their papers as subscription prices increase. Today, the sales amount to about half of the revenue of the newspapers in Germany (BDZV 2009) – a high share compared to many other countries. Challengers to these market structures are fended off rather aggressively, as could be seen when foreign investors tried to introduce free sheets in German metro areas. Local publishers immediately fought back with their own free papers and withdrew them again once the invader had been finished off.

This infrastructure helps make the German media system less vulnerable to economic pressures. The German media are less commercialised and less exposed to the vagaries of the stockmarket and pressures from private equity investors. Publishers can count on relatively stable streams of revenues thanks to the solid division of the market. But this comfortable situation may be a disadvantage in the long run: publishers have become used to high profits and may not yet be sufficiently under pressure to appreciate the need for future-oriented innovations.

Journalism under pressure

The current worldwide economic crisis hit the German industry hard. It led to a cut-back in advertising expenditure by companies and, in 2009, led to rapid falls in advertising revenues for the German media. While this is worrying for publishing houses, more relevant for the future prospects of journalism will be other more long-term developments. Journalism faces challenges arising from three broader processes. The first concerns the revolution in communication technology based on digitalisation and new networks of communication. The development of digital TV and radio, the internet and new mobile devices for receiving and exchanging news offer opportunities for journalism to become free of the traditional time and space constraints of public communication and to interact with its audiences. At the same time, the economic model of commercial journalism is undermined. The second challenge is a broader process of social change that (using the new technologies available) drives young audiences away from the traditional mass media. And the third challenge is the broader process of commercialisation that turns journalism into a business that is more than anything else oriented towards satisfying investors' needs rather than providing public goods. All three processes together interact with the current economic crisis and put journalism under pressure. In order to explore the nature of the crisis, we will first examine the audience for journalism in Germany; then we analyse the revenues sustaining commercial media organisations; finally we examine how commercial logic is pushing journalism towards crisis.

Pressure 1: media usage trends and the special role of the internet

The search for crisis symptoms in journalism in Germany might naturally start by investigating whether journalism is losing its audience. So far, this is not the case but there are changes in patterns of media use which may become a problem for traditional mass media in the long term.

A comprehensive report on communication and media commissioned by the German government found an 'impressive stability in the usage of traditional media'. Over the years, the time spent on media consumption in general has increased, with a growing trend of parallel use of different media (Hans-Bredow-Institut 2008: 373). As can be seen from Table 4.1, the general patterns of media use have remained fairly constant between 1999 and 2009. Looking at usage, television is the leading medium with regard to daily reach and time spent watching. Daily newspapers continue to reach more than 70 per cent of the population (Hans-Bredow-Institut 2008: 369–71). Not surprisingly, the internet is more widely used and has become part of the daily media repertoire of many people, but as Table 4.1 illustrates in terms of both the percentage reached among the German audience and average time of usage it cannot yet compete with the traditional media; 43 per cent of Germans think that the daily newspaper is the most credible source of information, followed by public TV and radio; online services come last at 6 per cent (data from 2004 as reported in BDZV 2009: 376).

A crisis for the traditional media might nevertheless be lurking under the surface of seemingly stable patterns of media use. There is a slow erosion of the reach of the daily newspaper, even though there was the comparatively high level of more than 70 per cent market reach and an average of 20 million copies sold per day in 2009. Nevertheless, press readership has been slowly eroding since the late 1980s. Different types of newspapers are affected to different degrees: while the tabloid *Bild* lost one and a half million buyers in the last decade, national quality dailies and weeklies defended their position, and in a few cases (*Die Zeit*) even expanded their reader base (Table 4.1).

The general losses cannot be blamed on the rise of the internet exclusively, as newspapers started to lose readers much earlier, parallel with the rise of commercial television and changing lifestyles of the young. The group of 14 to 19 year olds has a drastically different media repertoire from the average German media user (Hans-Bredow-Institut 2008: 373). German teenagers spend ten minutes reading a newspaper as opposed to 123 minutes surfing the internet per day. There is a clear age gap emerging, with under 30 year olds using less print and more digital media. Therefore, print is not replaced by web usage, in the sense that people are quitting their print subscriptions in order to get their news from the web. Web users are younger than the print audience and they grew up with the internet as their primary source of interaction among their peers and – to a much lesser degree – as source of news. Whether the younger cohorts will ever come back to printed media – or grow a habit of daily news consumption – is an open question. For now the comforting news for German newspapers publishers is that, even among the under 30s, every second person regularly reads newspapers and that there is a core group of highly educated and well-paid readers below 30 who read the paper as much as the older age groups do. In addition to reading the paper they also make intensive use of other media channels including the web (Köcher 2009: 116).

Table 4.1. Major news outlets and their market share in Germany – ten year trend

Average Daily Media Use: Minutes Spent (Daily reach)	1999	2009
Newspapers	30[a] (78%)	28[c] (71%)
TV	203[a] (73%)[a]	228 (71%)
Radio	205[a] (79%)[a]	182 (76%)
Internet	17[a] (29%/month)[a]	70 (48%)

Print Market: Circulation Sold in Millions (Daily reach)	1999	2009
Daily newspaper sector	24 (78%)	20 (71%)
Regional newspaper sector	n/a (68%)	14 (59%)
Tabloid newspaper sector	6 (21%)[a]	4 (21%)

Selected Flagship Newspapers: Paid Circulation Per Day, Mo-Fr, in Thousand[e]	1999	2009
Süddeutsche Zeitung (Munich, quality daily)	424	417
Frankfurter Allgemeine Zeitung (Frankfurt, quality daily)	417	365
BILD (Berlin, tabloid daily)	4446	3075
Der Spiegel (Hamburg, weekly news magazine)	1050[f]	1016
Die Zeit (Hamburg, weekly newspaper)	496[f]	502
Westdeutsche Allgemeine Zeitung (largest regional daily)	875[f]	819

Television Market: Minutes Per Day (Share of Daily TV Consumption)	1999	2009
ARD (largest public channel)	26 (14.2%)	26 (12.7%)
ZDF (second largest public channel)	24 (13.2%)	26 (12.6%)
Regional (all regional public channels combined)	25 (13%)[b]	28 (13.5%)
RTL (largest commercial channel)	27 (14.8%)	26 (12.3%)
SAT.1 (second largest commercial channel)	20 (10.8%)	22 (10.5%)
ProSieben (third largest commercial channel)	16 (8.4%)	14 (6.5%)

Data: Media Perspektiven Basisdaten 2000, 2005, 2009; BDZV 2009; ARD/ZDF-Onlinestudie; Langzeitstudie Massenkommunikation 2000, 2005. Notes: a= data refer to the year 2000; b= data refer to the year 2001; c= data refer to the year 2005; d= data refer to the year 2008; e= IVW 1/1999 and 4/2009; f= IVW 1/2008

Pressure 2: revenue trends and the special role of advertising

High profits are not something that one expects from a publishing house these days, but for Axel Springer AG the first quarter of 2010 saw profits rising to a record 18 per cent return on investment (EBITDA margin). This example illustrates that the situation of the printed press is not as dire as in other Western countries. Print revenues are under pressure due to losses in advertising, particularly in the classifieds market, but both advertising and sales revenues are still strong. In fact, hardly any other countries in the world generate higher incomes from advertising and sales than the German press does (WAN 2009: 57–9).

In 2008, the economic crisis led to a severe fall in advertising investment and revenues. Overall, the media's share of the advertising budget was heavily affected by this downswing. The net advertising income of the media fell by 2 per cent in 2008 and by another 10 per cent (€2 billion) in 2009, arriving at €18.4 billion net advertising (ZAW 2010). Furthermore, the printed media are losing market shares. Newspapers' share of total advertising expenditures fell from 48.1 per cent in 1998 to 37 per cent in 2008 (WARC 2008). The internet share has been rising – from a 0.2 per cent share in 1998 to 15 per cent in 2008 (WARC 2008). Projections show that if the current trends in the ad market, reader market and in newspapers' cost structure continue unchanged, the German newspaper industry will accumulate a deficit of more than €2 billion by the year 2018 (Kollo 2010: 12). Doing nothing is thus not an option. The German newspaper press may still be in a relatively comfortable position today but the existing business model is clearly threatened in the long term.

Pressure 3: management trends and the special role of profit expectations

Printed newspapers are less profitable than before. This is not necessarily a problem given that profit margins of more than 10 per cent used to be the norm in the German press and publishers believing in public service might be able to tolerate a few percentage points less. Also, large publishing houses with cross-media platforms like Springer and Bertelsmann compensate losses of their daily newspapers with gains in other segments of their portfolio. Falling profits may seem less tolerable for those publishers who are predominantly interested in high profits. It is obvious that, with the change from the founders' generation to their heirs, the commercial logic has become more dominant in many publishing houses. Newspapers long in family hands have been sold to investors who seem to be in the business only for the money. Some of the recent investors in the German media market based their acquisitions on debt which they were no longer able to service in times of economic crisis (Riesterer and Wittrock 2009). Further cut-backs were the result. Therefore, not all current troubles can be blamed on the internet; some are the result of failed investment, management decisions and unrealistic profit expectations.

To briefly sum up the discussion so far: journalism in Germany is better financed and the daily press still in a stronger position than in some other countries. The regional press continues to be firmly embedded in their communities; subscription and home delivery systems are advanced. German audiences seem loyal to their traditional media. Taking all channels together, German media reach more people today than ever before. There are, however, pressures that will aggravate in the long term: the loss of a significant part of the younger audience for traditional media and the shrinking share of a stagnating advertising market. Profit margins from the golden age of the printed press will not return. Lower profits and losses due to years of economic crisis will turn into a problem for journalism if media managers insist on double-digit profit margins and if they continue to cut down the resources for producing quality journalism.

Media business responses: between cutting costs and embracing change

The set of possible business responses by media organisations to save accountability journalism comprise at least five options. The first two strategies are aimed at cutting costs: by slashing resources or restructuring editorial processes. A third response aims at winning audiences through new communication channels, modernised formats, or innovative contents. Two final response strategies rely on developing new business models that either complement or replace existing models. While some of these responses focus on reducing costs in order to compensate for declining revenues, others focus on the challenge of winning younger audiences or on embracing the new possibilities of digital communication. The responses are separated for the purpose of analysis but are closely intertwined in practice.

Response 1: saving money by cutting back resources

During both downturns of the media economy in the last decade (one starting in 2001 and the other in 2008) the default response to diminished revenues was to cut costs. This affected administrative resources and the technical process of producing the newspaper but, more importantly for the quality of journalism, also the newsroom.

From 2000 to 2009 about 1,000 full-time journalists on German newspapers lost their jobs, reducing the total number from 15,300 to 14,300 (Keller 2009: 106). Longitudinal data on the journalistic workforce are available from a two-wave representative survey conducted in 1993 and 2005. It finds that, in spite of an expanding media landscape with growing online journalism, additional TV and radio stations, and new special-interest magazines, the overall number of full-time journalists in Germany shrank from 54,000 to 48,000 (Weischenberg et al. 2006). The decrease mostly concerned freelance journalists who are not as well protected by German employment laws as journalists on fixed contracts.

While not every job that is cut will affect the quality of the content, it is plausible to assume that the accumulated effect has implications for overall performance. The closure of local bureaux in regions that are not served by other papers reduces the accountability of local politicians. Therefore, the strategy of cutting down journalism will affect the working of democracy in some areas while it might indeed be compensated by more efficiency or new forms of journalism in other areas, as will be shown below.

Response 2: getting more efficient by restructuring journalism

The second approach to saving costs tries to avoid downsizing journalism. The aim is to become more efficient by restructuring the newsroom. The promises of synergies between different sections, departments, and editions have encouraged a trend towards integrated newsrooms (Brüggemann 2002). In order to streamline editorial processes, centralised newsrooms have been widely introduced, which also created new work profiles following closer the Anglo-Saxon model of a separation between editors and reporters (Esser 1998). Then, the gains in efficiency thanks to new structures are used to reduce costs (for example by laying off journalists) rather than reinvesting the freed resources into improving journalistic output.

Studies of the streamlining of the journalistic work process and how this affects the quality of the content are scarce and most rely on interviews with journalists rather than analysing the actual changes in content production and outcome. Journalists in the newly integrated newsrooms admit that the reforms enhanced the quality of their newspapers and also their job satisfaction, in spite of working longer hours under increased time pressures (Schneider 2009). On the other hand, there are fears about the superficiality of 'assembly line journalism' which is more concerned with formatting content for different outlets than with thorough investigation and thoughtful reflection (Neininger-Schwarz 2010).

The introduction of centralised news desks and new work profiles may enhance the efficiency of the product. If it goes hand in hand with scaling down the number of regional offices and laying off journalists, it might also result in lower standards of accountability in the German media, but in the absence of broader empirical studies on the topic, it is too early to rush to conclusions about the democratic impact of the changing structures of many newsrooms in Germany.

Response 3: gaining audiences with new media outlets, formats, and contents

Newspaper managers have responded to the pressures of shrinking audiences, especially amongst the young, by giving their products a face-lift and upgrading their user value. This resulted in new formats and new contents. Virtually all German media outlets have pursued this strategy to some degree. Newspapers have been relaunched, with colour and pictures. Some have downsized the format to tabloid size and many have strengthened their web presence. Despite this, web features and interaction with users and citizen journalists are not fully embraced by German media organisations. This is especially true for the websites of daily newspapers. In 2007, only 3 per cent of the internet editions of German newspapers produced significant amounts of exclusive web content (Neuberger *et al.* 2009: 178). In 2009, fewer than half of German newspaper websites allowed users to comment on articles (Büffel and Schumacher 2010) – the most basic feature of integrating user-generated content. By the end of 2009, it was still the exception for German media outlets to offer an iPhone application. (This changed somewhat around the 2010 football World Cup.)

For quality online journalism, there is only one success story to be told: *Spiegel Online* is Germany's most lucrative and admired example of a traditional print medium going online and establishing a new brand. Following a strategy of an autonomous web edition with 60 journalists, it attracts 5.6 million unique visitors per month. There is little overlap between the regular online readers and those of the printed magazine *Der Spiegel. Spiegel Online* is the most frequently quoted German online outlet, an extremely influential agenda setter, and said to have been profitable since 2005. It is considered the best example in Germany of how new communication channels can win additional audiences for traditional media brands. It entail investment in the interactive potential of digital journalism and has also made the printed edition of *Der Spiegel* more relevant in a multi-channel environment.

Response 4: new or alternative business models

New sources of revenue are another way out of the quagmire faced by commercial media outlets. These revenues might stem from higher subscription prices, fees for online content, or cross-subsidies from other commercial activities such as selling books, DVDs, or educational travel. Apart from these new sources of income to complement the financial model of commercial media, there are a number of alternative models of media ownership which have a longstanding tradition in the German quality press.

As in other countries, fees for online news have not gained much traction in Germany, while higher subscription rates for newspapers have been successfully implemented and have compensated for some of the losses on the advertising side. Selling book series and DVDs as well as different types of promotional material (including bikes and coffee in the case of the Berlin-based *Tageszeitung*) has become commonplace among German publishing houses.

While these measures are not specific to the German case, the presence of a number of successful alternative ownership models might be interesting from a comparative perspective:

- The daily newspaper *Frankfurter Allgemeine Zeitung* (*FAZ*) is owned by the independent FAZIT-Foundation, a non-profit foundation aiming to promote science, research, and education.

- The weekly newsmagazine *Der Spiegel* is majority-owned by its employees who are the shareholders.

- The daily newspaper *Die Tageszeitung* (*taz*) is co-operative-owned and administrated by the workers' self-management.

- The leading news agency Deutsche Presse Agentur (dpa) is established as a limited liability company, jointly owned by German media organisations.

These alternative models of ownership may help ensure that the interest in short-term gains does not dominate over the interest in quality journalism and long-term success. They do not prevent newspapers from being forced to trim resources if advertising revenues or subscription rates go down but they guarantee that a genuine interest in journalism prevails over the commercial interest in return on invest. Profit margins close to zero might be tolerable for a foundation but not so for commercial investors.

Response 5: new media ventures complementing traditional journalism

If traditional media remain unable to adapt to the changing needs of the audience and the digital media environment, new ventures might help invigorate and complement traditional journalism. Blogs, newly founded not-for-profit organisations offering journalistic content and pro-am collaborations between journalists and citizens might be examples of these new ventures in the media market. In the German case, however, new outlets outside the traditional media universe have not yet really succeeded in gaining a substantial audience or more than episodic significance for public debates.

The *Netzeitung* was probably the most ambitious project to establish independent web journalism in Germany. Founded in 2000 as the first online-only newspaper in Germany (pure player), it survived several changes in ownership which mostly resulted in further budget cuts until in 2009 the last fourteen journalists were laid off in order to turn the 'newspaper' into an automated news portal. While the *Netzeitung* had some success in providing quality journalism on the web, it never really managed to establish itself as a brand that could compete with *Spiegel Online* or other web outlets of traditional news media.

While *Netzeitung* was mainly a failed attempt at making profits with web journalism, a number of blogs have gained some relevance for local or special interest publics. Germany's best known blog, *Bildblog*, was founded in 2004 and specialises in media critique. It provides a daily commentary on the shortcomings of the tabloid *Bild*. In 2009 the concept was expanded into a more general media-watch blog that goes beyond the missteps of *Bild*. Another much-observed blog is *Wir-in-NRW*, which focuses on critical coverage of local and regional politics in the state of North-Rhine-Westfalia. Together with other local blogs like *Ruhrbarone* they pick up important stories neglected by the dominant regional newspaper *WAZ* which laid off 300 out of its 900 journalists in 2009.

In order to gain nation-wide significance these blogs depend, however, on the traditional news media to take up their stories. Compared to the US, the German media landscape has not created new players comparable in reach to, for example, the *Huffington Post*. One reason for this is the still relatively high credibility of established media brands. These traditional news organisations launched extensive and professional online platforms early on, leaving little room in the German web sphere for alternative outlets. New players only have a chance if they find manifest voids not filled by traditional media.

In sum, our review finds that all five business responses are embraced to some extent but the smaller scope of the crisis and more stable market structures have put less pressure on publishers to invest in innovative forms of journalism. The current challenges have nevertheless triggered a broader debate in media and policy circles about how to improve the general framework conditions of the German press so that it can grow out of the current difficulties stronger and fitter.

Media policy responses

The expectation that the German government has an institutional responsibility for creating framework conditions that allow the press to thrive and fulfil its functions for democracy follows from Article 5 of the German constitution (*Grundgesetz*) which states that 'Freedom of the press and freedom of reporting by radio and television are guaranteed'. Of the many possible policy responses some will never be adopted (even if considered elsewhere) while others are already being implemented, as the following overview shows.

Response 1: direct state aid

Direct state aid or financial emergence measures like that employed in France ('États Généraux de Presse') or discussed in the USA ('Newspaper Revitalisation Act') are considered out of the question by the German government and by the newspaper publishers' associations. Such measures, they say, would violate the sacred principle of separating government and press demanded by the constitution. It is worth noting that neither the local press nor the high-quality national press has requested any kind of financial assistance. Another idea that has been flat-out rejected by both government and big publishers is that of a public service press fund. Such a fund – financed by a public fee to support newspapers based on the quality of their content and their contribution to a democratic public sphere – was proposed by German philosopher Jürgen Habermas in 2007. It is a renewal of an idea that was first proposed in the 1970s. As in the past, the idea finds few backers today.[1] Critics say that independent newspapers cannot be regulated by public law.

---

[1] There are more proposals that have been floating around without a serious chance of getting adopted, such as the Green Party's idea of a 'cultural flat rate' tax on broadband subscriptions, the proceeds of which would be used to underwrite quality content.

Response 2: indirect state aid

Indirect state aid refers, for example, to reduced postal rates or preferred tax treatment for the newspaper industry. The German Newspaper Publisher Association (BDZV) demanded in 2009 a further reduction in VAT rate for press products from the current rate of 7 per cent. In 2010 the BDZV softened its stance by demanding that this rate should at least not be increased.

Other indirect state support measures, like funds to improve local journalism or subsidise new online news ventures, or funds to help media organisations modernise their technological equipment and teach their journalists multimedia skills, are not on the policy agenda.

A final issue of indirect state aid is related to Germany's public service broadcasting system. The main source of funding for ARD and ZDF is a broadcast fee (constituting 85 per cent of the revenue), complemented by income from advertising and sponsorship (5 per cent) and other income such as co-productions (10 per cent).[2] The use of broadcast fee revenue to subsidise 'press-like texts' on the websites of ARD and ZDF was ruled 'illegal state aid' by the European Commission in 2006. This resulted in a new law which – in compliance with EU regulations – imposes stricter conditions on German public service broadcasters with regard to using public funding for online activities (see below).

Response 3: reforming legal framework conditions to improve competitiveness and revenue structures

Media policy responses in Germany focus less on granting state aid and more on improving general framework conditions for the press. Government politicians have been receptive to the demands of the German Newspaper Publishers Association to make changes to the Act against Restraints of Competition (*Gesetz gegen Wettbewerbsbeschränkungen*), the Media Merger and Acquisitions Act (*Pressefusionsgesetz*), Copyright Law (*Urheberrechtsgesetz*), and related intellectual property rights. Publishers argue that in a converged context some old rules have become outdated and some new ones have become necessary. The following policy changes are currently debated.

- Lift restrictions on mergers between newspapers in neighbouring markets if they do not compete for the same readers.

- Lift the threshold value from currently €25 million to €100 million for mergers between media companies that can go ahead without going through an investigation and approval process by the Federal Cartel Office.

- Lift restrictions on cross-media acquisitions, enabling newspapers to cooperate actively with local or regional radio and television.

[2] As institutions under public law, ARD and ZDF are state-owned but independent of government control. The broadcasting fee is calculated by an independent commission (the KEF) and then approved of by the German parliament. Every citizen who owns a receiving device is required to register it with a fee collection centre (the GEZ) set up and run by the public broadcasters. PSB's independence from politics is not all-encompassing. For example, all major parties are represented in the supervising broadcast councils of both ARD and ZDF. This has sometimes led to politicized hiring decisions for key journalistic personnel.

- Lift restrictions on joint operating agreements entered into by two or more newspapers in which the print facilities or distribution operations are merged, although each business retains its status as a separate entity in terms of profits and individual mission.

Of special importance to German newspaper publishers is government support in helping them protect their online news content from what they consider 'unlawful use' by search engines, news aggregators, and other commercial operators without consent or compensation. The German Minister of Justice supports the introduction of a new so-called neighbouring right ('Leistungsschutzrecht') that would give content providers more control over their material. In spring 2010 publisher associations and journalist unions were invited to draft legislation that would protect the intellectual creation of value by authors and publishers more effectively. The draft proposes a right similar to protections that already exist for music publishers and other content owners. With the adoption of two new paragraphs in the German Copyright Law (paragraphs 87f and 87g, *Urheberrechtsgesetz*), web aggregators like Google News would be required to compensate content providers for any commercial use of published material online. This would be done against payment of a licence fee to a special collecting agency. Several such agencies in charge of gathering and distributing royalty fees do exist already in Germany (like VG Wort) and could be used for this purpose. Private, non-commercial use of news articles would remain unrestricted and not fall under this law. A core goal would be to secure revenue for news reporting online. While this draft law has already been criticised by news aggregators and free-internet advocates and still has many legal loopholes to fill, the German government has made it clear that it intends to act – not only at the national but also the European level where the EC Copyright Directive would need to be adapted too. The conflict between search engines, news aggregators, and publishers continues to brew, but the real threat of legal action may bring them to the negotiating table.

Response 4: curtailing the privileged position of public service broadcasters

German government politicians have also responded positively to revising the Interstate Broadcasting Treaty (*Rundfunkstaatsvertrag*) which regulates the funding system and the guidelines for online activities and advertising on public service television channels. One proposal is to further restrict online activities by public broadcasters. The private broadcasters are concerned about distortion of competition and 'press-like' content funded by broadcast fees, the demand for which could also be met by the commercial providers. According to a 2008 revision of Germany's Interstate Broadcasting Treaty – made necessary after intervention by the European Commission – the main public broadcasters ARD and ZDF are already required to undertake a three-step test with respect to their online offerings to check whether there is indeed 'public value' in any planned new-media service, and to what extent these services may unnecessarily damage the commercial offerings by private media companies (*Drei-Stufen-Tests fuer Telemedien der öffentlich-rechtlichen Rundfunkanstalten*).[3] Furthermore, the German

---

[3] This three-step test (loosely comparable to the Public Value Test in Great Britain) must provide evidence that the added value of a proposed new media offering contributes to the public service; must involve consultation of interested parties and commercial competitors; and must receive approval by the governing broadcasting councils of the public channels and by a round of independent experts.

Culture Secretary and other politicians complained in spring 2010 that elaborate online and mobile offerings by public broadcasters (like iPhone apps for news clips) cause unfair competition to commercial news entities and pose a threat to Germany's diverse newspaper press. All these details need to be decided on soon since the next revision of the Interstate Broadcasting Treaty will take effect on 1 January 2013.

Implications for democracy

For many observers, the biggest enemy of a free and democratic press is not the government or the state but managers and market conditions of the media world itself. High-profile newspaper journalists and unions have recently been warning of deteriorating working conditions and fewer resources to carry out the core function of news journalism: independent reporting that provides reliable information, in-depth investigation and thorough analysis that can help create an informed and engaged citizenry (Prantl 2009). This is close to what Downie and Schudson (2009) have called 'accountability journalism'. They link it to the watchdog function of the press and define it as 'reporting that holds government officials accountable to the legal and moral standards of public service and keeps business and professional leaders accountable to society's expectations of integrity and fairness' (Downie and Schudson 2009: 9). Accountability journalism in Germany grew to healthy levels in the 1960s and 1970s and has stayed stable until today without grave disruptions or existential threats. With regard to the current situation we conclude that Germany suffers neither from a general media crisis nor from a crisis of democracy. At most it suffers from a newspaper publishing crisis. This, however, is at least partly a self-inflicted crisis. The current situation is best described as a 'strategic crisis for newspaper publishers'. This strategic crisis reveals that a substantial part of the German press industry has not been capable, or willing, to innovate their publishing model in time (Jarren 2009).

There is definitely no crisis of democracy because never in its history have the citizens of Germany been informed so fully and in such a cost-effective fashion by such a diverse range of national and international sources. Many German newspapers reach more readers than ever before when online and offline audiences are combined. The public service broadcasting system provides a comprehensive and high-quality programme. However, one core media segment with respect to accountability journalism, namely the quality press, faces financial difficulty and painful readjustment to a multi-channel environment in which they may lose their once influential position as the dominant news providers. But they will cope better than many American papers because they are more firmly rooted in the regions, are an integral part of the German reading culture, and benefit from a widely shared consensus that there is a civic duty to keep informed. German papers maintain efficient home delivery operations and profit from relatively high subscription rates. They are much less exposed to investors and financial speculators and suffer less competition from talk radio and bloggers. They have not radically thinned out their national and international coverage, have not hopelessly lost the younger generation, and are still valued and appreciated by the opinion-leading elites and large parts of the general public. What the German newspaper press faces is a kind of classic structural adjustment not dissimilar to other 'traditional' industries like steel, coal, or agriculture which at some point all had to adapt to new contexts and conditions.

The second reason why Germany does not experience a crisis of democracy stems from the insight that democracy requires publishers or journalists only to the extent that their presence is necessary to sustain an informed, unrestrained, and stimulated public sphere – wherever and however it is constituted. At many places in the World Wide Web we see a public sphere evolving without professional journalists. When looking for manifestations of rationality, deliberation, and orientation for citizens one could argue that online spaces like Wikipedia, open-source software projects, or ambitious blogs are indeed examples of rational, coordinated, and multi-filtered discourse whose end products can easily compete with the average newspaper article. But it is clear that the internet does not offer two crucial things: first, in-depth and costly investigations that hold powerful interests accountable and do not falter at the first hurdle; and second, a continued and reliable provision of independent reporting on current affairs that helps create an informed and engaged citizenry. To provide these services, journalism is needed, but not necessarily in the form of commercially driven enterprises. The German state acknowledges the importance of journalism for a democratic public sphere. This is why it maintains Europe's largest public service broadcasting system, financed with over €7 billion per year, and subjects it to a statutory remit that lists detailed programme expectations.

Nevertheless, it is obvious that traditional publishers and quality-oriented media organisations are under pressure and in need of advice about how to overcome their strategy crisis. Here we are not principally against the involvement of media regulators and policy initiatives *as long as* this involvement is clearly and securely aimed at supporting innovation, quality, and public service (see Jarren 2010). Fostering journalistic innovation and excellence may require intellectual and (indirect) material support; what this support should ideally look like is very hard to say. We do see that the German press, by and large, shows a clear commitment to quality journalism. And we also see many papers still standing strong. German publishers are extremely well organised and connected, and fight resolutely for more favourable framework conditions at all levels. This includes standing up to what they perceive as an over-extravagant online appetite of public broadcasters and global web aggregators. Yet some of their policy desires seem to us to go too far, especially with regard to public broadcasters. Before developing a larger-scheme solution, publishing houses would have to rethink their profit expectations and social responsibility. We conclude by saying that the current 'crisis' is less severe in Germany than in some other countries. It might still cause trouble for some papers and even lead to a moderate downsizing of the media landscape but this will do no significant harm to German democracy.

This brings us to the final question of how some of the publishers' media policy proposals discussed above should be evaluated from a democratic-normative perspective. First, let us note that policy proposals that are directed at extending copyright laws in order to protect publishers from the commercial use of published material online (Google News) or the non-commercial use of published material online ('file sharing piracy') run counter to the spirit of openness that characterises the web. These policy proposals have little value for the consumer or the health of democracy but offer substantial financial benefit for publishers who have trouble finding workable business models for the digital age. We conclude that a free democracy requires access to free and unlimited information, but we also acknowledge a need to ensure that there is a way to pay for the production of this content. This brings us to our second point. Policy proposals aimed at loosening anti-trust laws play into the hands of free-market advocates. Yet concentration of media power in the hands of a few is fundamentally at odds with basic democratic values. It can threaten diverse public discourse; it can increase the likelihood of owners using their media power for political reasons; and it can make owners more interested in generating profit than providing quality journalism. On the other hand it is clear that the production of quality information is expensive, requires effort, time, devotion, and money – resources that very small enterprises cannot always provide. Therefore, large media companies are not problematic for democracy as such. They are problematic if they threaten the plurality of public debates and if they are exclusively guided by a logic of maximising profits at the cost of providing quality journalism. The risk of a commercial logic dominating the public interest is inherent in all commercial enterprises. Therefore, it would be detrimental to democracy to severely restrict the room for manoeuvre for public broadcasting, for example by drastically restricting its online activities. Strong public broadcasting and a strong commercial media market should live side by side in a stable media ecology in which media policy regulation sees its role as enabling and rewarding the provision of quality content.

References

ARD/ZDF (2010) *ARD/ZDF Online Studie*. www.ard-zdf-onlinestudie.de (29 June).

BDZV Bundesverband Deutscher Zeitungsverleger (2009) *Zeitungen 2009*. Berlin: BDZV.

Brüggemann, M. (2002) *The Missing Link: Crossmediale Vernetzung von Print und Online. Fallstudien führender Print Medien in Deutschland und den USA*. Munich: Verlag Reinhard Fischer.

Büffel, S. and P. Schumacher (2010) 'Weg ins Social Web', *Medium Magazin*, 1/2: 32–3.

Dreier, H. (2009) 'Das Mediensystem Deutschlands', in Hans-Bredow-Institut (ed.), *Internationales Handbuch Medien*. Baden-Baden: Nomos, 257–72.

Downie, L. Jr. and M. Schudson (2009) 'The Reconstruction of American Journalism', *Columbia Journalism Review* (Nov./Dec.).

Esser, F. (1998) 'Editorial Structures and Work Principles in British and German Newsrooms', *European Journal of Communication*, 13(3): 375–406.

Hans-Bredow-Institut (2008) *Zur Entwicklung der Medien in Deutschland zwischen 1998 und 2007: Wissenschaftliches Gutachten zum Kommunikations- und Medienbericht der Bundesregierung*. Hamburg: Hans-Bredow-Institut; www.hans-bredow-institut. de/de/forschung/kommunikations-medienbericht-bundesregierung (20 July).

Jarren, O. (2009) 'Pressekrise, Medienkrise, Demokratiekrise?' Key note speech at the 8th Communication Day in Biel (in German), 20 Oct.

— (2010) 'Krise der Eliten', *EPD Medien*, 39 (22 May): 22–8.

Keller, D. (2009) 'Schwierige Zeiten: Zur wirtschaftlichen Lage der deutschen Zeitungen', in BDZV (ed.), *Zeitungen 2009*, 29–108.

Köcher, R. (2009) 'Beschränkte Suche statt breiter Lektüre: Wie das Internet die Gesellschaft verändert', in BDZV (ed.), *Zeitungen 2009*, 109–24.

Kolo, C. (2010) 'Zeitungskrise und Zeitungszukunft: Modellierung von Entwicklungsszenarien vor dem Hintergrund verschiedener Subventionierungsvorschläge', in Hardy G. (ed.), *Public Value in der Digital- und Internetökonomie*. Cologne: Herbert von Halem Verlag.

Media Perspektiven (2000, 2005, 2009) *Basisdaten: Daten zur Mediensituation in Deutschland*. Frankfurt: Media Perspektiven.

Neininger-Schwarz, N. (2010) 'Der Journalist am Fließband', *Neue Zürcher Zeitung*,

50 (5 Jan.).

Neuberger, C., C. Nuernbergk, and M. Rischke (2009) 'Journalismus im Internet: Zwischen Profession, Partizipation und Technik', *Media Perspektiven*, 4: 174–88.

Prantl, H. (2009) 'Sind Zeitungen systemrelevant?' Key note speech at the Annual Meeting of the investigative journalism network Netzwerk Recherche in Hamburg (in German), 6 June.

Reitze, H. and C. Ridder (2005) *Massenkommunikation VII: Eine Langzeitstudie zur Mediennutzung und Medienbewertung 1964–2005*. Baden-Baden: Nomos 2006.

Riesterer, F. and O. Wittrock (2009) 'Sparfalle: Die Wirtschaftskrise und eigenen Fehler machen den Medien zu schaffen', *Journalist*, 1: 12–17.

Röper, H. (2008) 'Konzentrationssprung im Markt der Tageszeitungen', *Media Perspektiven*, 8: 420–37.

Schneider, V. (2009) 'Alle Nachrichten über einen Tisch', *Message*, 1: 80–3.

WAN (2009) *World Press Trends 2009*. Paris: World Association of Newspapers.

WARC (2008) *World Advertising Trends 2008*. Oxford: World Advertising Research Center.

Weischenberg, Siegfried, Maja Malik, and Armin Scholl (2006) 'Journalismus in Deutschland 2005', *Media Perspektiven*, 7: 346–61.

ZAW Zentralverband der Deutschen Werbewirtschaft (2010) *Medien verlieren 2 Milliarden Werbe-Euro netto: Werbemarkt sackt um 6 Prozent*; www.zaw.de/index. php?menuid=119

5. The Unravelling Finnish Media Policy Consensus?

Hannu Nieminen

Introduction

Recent years have been extremely testing for the whole media business. Traditional news journalism, anchored historically in such concepts as public interest and social values, is increasingly treated as one commodity among others. Journalism is deeply affected by technological advances – the expansion of broadband internet, the advance of digital television, the growth of mobile communications, and so on. In this article I will provide a brief overview of the developments in Finland, and ask four questions. What have been the key pressures facing journalism? How has the media industry reacted to these pressures? What has been the response by policy-makers? And how does this all relate to wider developments in Finnish society?

The media have been an elemental part of the Finnish social contract and they enjoy the status of national institutions.[1] This is reflected in the whole structure of the Finnish media system – from newspapers and electronic media to telecommunications. From the 1990s the Finnish social contract, however, has suffered from increasing problems, which have also been reflected in the media. Media policy has been influenced by more general European trends of deregulation and marketisation (see e.g. van Cuilenburg and McQuail 2003; Harcourt 2005; Michalis 2007), which has weakened not only the position of YLE (the Finnish Broadcasting Company), but also the newspaper press, which has suffered from the axing of the public press subsidies (Herkman 2009).

A central characteristic of Nordic societies is their strong literary culture: reading is historically highly valued. This can still be clearly seen in Finland where the newspaper readership figures, although steadily declining, are still among the highest in the world (more than 400 copies per 1,000 population, or more than twice the figure in for example France or the United States.

At the same time, Finland – as the home country of Nokia Corporation – has been an early adopter of new information and communication technologies (ICTs).

---

[1] Finland is geographically a large country (330.000 km²) but, with a population of only 5.5 million, it is one of Europe's most sparsely populated countries. Most people speak Finnish, but there is also an influential Swedish-speaking minority (5% of population).

Since 1995, the notion of the 'Information Society' has held a central position in Finnish governmental policies.[2] One landmark was the full digitalisation of Finnish television broadcasting as the first European country to do so in 2007. The digital television network covers 99.9 per cent of the country. The government is committed to providing a 100 Mbit/s broadband connection to all households by 2015. The next national information society strategy for 2011–14 is currently being developed.

Nordic societies are often called 'social democracies', not only because of their model of social welfare, but also because of the strong position that social democratic parties have historically enjoyed in these countries. From the 1990s onwards, however, they have lost much of their influence. In Finland, a major political shift took place in the parliamentary elections in 2007 when the Social Democratic Party was left in third place behind the Centre Party (agrarian centre) and National Coalition Party (conservative). The formation of a centre-right government meant a shift in economic and cultural policies, as market values increasingly substituted for social and democratic values in governmental strategies.

The Finnish media system in the 2000s

The Finnish media system in the 2000s can briefly be characterised by four main features.

High level of concentration

As in many small countries, the media market in Finland is dominated by few players. In newspaper publishing, the top four companies have 75 per cent of the market; in magazines, the big four have some 77 per cent market share (according to data from Statistics Finland). One company (Sanoma Group) has an exceptionally central position: it controls a third of the total newspaper circulation (2008) and 32 per cent of magazine circulation; it owns a television channel (the third biggest in the country, with a 15 per cent audience share) and the biggest publishing house in Finland (45 per cent of the market for books), among other things.

Established division of markets

In Finland, there is only one major national newspaper (*Helsingin Sanomat*) with a circulation of about 400,000 copies in 2009. Additionally, all leading regional newspapers – about twenty-eight in all – are practically in a monopoly situation in their market areas. There is no major market competition except between the evening papers (tabloids) where two leading media houses fight fiercely, pitting the *Ilta-Sanomat* (152,948 copies) against the *Iltalehti* (112,778 copies). In the television market YLE has established a clear leading role, according to Finnpanel data (with 43 per cent audience share; commercial MTV3 has 25 per cent, and Sanoma's Nelonen has 15 per cent).

---

[2] The first national Information Society Strategy was adopted by the Finnish government as early as 1995.

A sound professional culture

The media, as national institutions, enjoy high public trust in Finland (EVA 2009a). Media professionals are today mostly well educated and they share a basic commitment to common quality standards. The Council for Mass Media in Finland (Julkisen Sanan Neuvosto, JSN) represents all main interest groups. Its members include representatives from media management as well as from journalists and different audience groups, and it follows commonly agreed ethical codes (*Journalistin ohjeet,* by the Finnish National Union of Journalists).

A profitable national media structure

There is a well-established three-tier newspaper structure between national, regional, and local papers. All these tiers have generally remained reasonably profitable even in the crisis year 2009 (e.g. the operating profit of Sanoma Group dropped from 11 per cent in 2008 to 9 per cent in 2009; the operating profit of Keskisuomalainen Group dropped from 20 per cent in 2008 to 16 per cent in 2009). Early home delivery of newspapers is available for 90 per cent of all households.

Key pressures facing news organisations and journalism in Finland

Despite its relative stability, in the last few years the media environment in Finland has changed in fundamental ways. Three main challenges have been the decline in newspaper readership, a big drop in advertising income, and the expansion of broadband internet connections.

The (slow) decline in newspaper readership

From the peak year 1989 the total circulation of newspapers has fallen some 20 per cent, although the decline has slowed down in the 2000s (see Table 5.1). According to recent statistics, the readership has actually slightly increased in 2008. The fall in circulation has obviously harmed the finances of the newspapers. In practical terms, income from sales and subscriptions has stayed on the same level for over ten years, whereas all other costs (printing, distribution, salaries) have steadily increased. For the future, the main problem is the reading habits of the young. Among people over 45 years old, more than 80 per cent read newspapers daily, and the average time spent reading is 35 minutes per day. Among those under 24, only some 56 per cent read newspapers daily and the average time is less than 15 minutes.

Table 5.1. Circulation of newspapers per 1,000 persons

	1998	2003	2008	Change 1998-2008
Dailies (7–4 issues/week)	455	430	400	-12%
Non-dailies (3–1 issues/week)	191	188	177	-7%
Total	646	619	577	-11%

Data: Statistics Finland 2010: 179.

A drop in advertising

As newspapers lose their economic basis, it hits news journalism hardest. Compared to 2008, in 2009 newspapers lost 22 per cent and television companies 12 per cent of their advertising income (see Table 5.2). This only adds to the longer decline in newspaper where the total drop in advertisement revenues between 2000 and 2009 was 38 per cent. Although online advertising increased to some extent, it did not benefit online news journalism as much as entertainment and other more commercially viable websites. The figures from early 2010 indicate that the trends are steady: advertising in newspapers and magazines continues to drop (January–April 2010, down respectively 2.3 and 8.6 per cent from 2009), as it increases for the internet and television (up respectively 19.2 and 4.3 per cent) (Markkinointi ja mainonta 2010). As the Finnish experience has confirmed too, people are not prepared to pay for online journalism. This means that news journalism is in dire straits: it loses money in print and it is not profitable online.

Table 5.2. Advertising in media 2008–2009 (million €)

	2008	2009	Change
Newspapers, total	604.5	474.2	-21.6%
Television, total	268.1	237.0	-11.6%
Online media, total	149.3	158.3	+6.0%
Media advertising, total	1499.8	1263.4	-15.8%

Data: Mainostajat.fi 2010.

The expansion of broadband internet connections

As elsewhere in Europe, broadband internet has expanded rapidly in Finland. From 2008 to 2009 the number of broadband connections increased by 18 per cent. However, although the government has actively promoted the large-scale deployment of ICT in both public and private sectors, progress has not been as fast and successful as hoped. In several information society indicators Finland is still lagging behind its Nordic neighbours. One of the main reasons appears to have been the blind trust in the ability of market forces to bring about all the benefits associated with the information society, without public-sector involvement. Even industry think-tanks like the Finnish Business and Policy Forum EVA now argue that this strategy has failed, and call for stronger governmental intervention (2009a). One major source of alarm is that internet use in Finland appears to have saturated or even declined: in 2008, 70 per cent of households recorded having an internet connection, whereas in 2009 the figure was 68 (Statistics Finland).

The responses of news organisations

As some of the challenges have been felt for a longer period, news organisations' responses include both long-term strategic and more immediate organisational and content-based reactions.

Pressure on YLE: distorting the market

As a reaction to the drop in advertising revenue, both print media and commercial TV companies have directed their criticism increasingly at the Finnish Broadcasting Company, YLE. In this situation, YLE's new strategy has been especially provocative to some. YLE offers its news freely not only through the internet but also by allowing it to be freely redistributed, for instance by commercially run electronic newsstands at railway stations and airports. Additionally, YLE has announced plans to extend its regional news services on the internet. Commercial media companies have filed an official complaint to the European Commission, arguing that YLE has violated EU state aid policy (GT-raportti 2010). From the viewpoint of commercial companies, the problem with YLE is that it has been able to profit from their problems and solidify its own market position in an increasingly competitive environment (see Table 5.3). The critical claims included that YLE provides content that would be commercially viable (like HBO programmes), and thus distorts the market. Additionally, as explained above, YLE is seen as exceeding its remit by developing new free online services which would compete unfairly with commercial services.

Table 5.3. Television: channel shares 2000–2009

	2000	2005	2007	2009
YLE	42%	44%	44%	44%
MTV3	41%	37%	33%	32%
Nelonen	12%	11%	12%	15%
Others	5%	8%	13%	10%

Data: Statistics Finland 2010, 79; Finnpanel 2010.

Representatives of the media industry have expressed their frustration with the YLE on several occasions. In brief, they want (Finnish Media Industry 2009):

- to cap YLE's spending so that it cannot unjustly benefit from the market situation; this means that there should be no increase in YLE's funding, based on the licence fee;

- to rewrite YLE's remit so that it cannot compete in light entertainment with commercial companies (YLE's concentration on 'its core content');

- to establish a control system which would allow the industry to have more say over YLE's programming policy.

New market for pay TV

Television broadcasting became fully digitalised in Finland in 2007. This transformed the business environment of Finnish commercial television fundamentally. Digitalisation broke down the earlier coexistence between the media companies as new channels were rapidly established. Digitalisation opened way for the commercial companies to start up a number of pay-channels – the number of households subscribing to pay-tv services rose in a few years from 5 per cent (in 2005) to 25 per cent (in 2008).

This means that, as pay TV offers commercial television companies new profitable sources of revenue, they are no longer as dependent on the advertising market as they have been (GT-raportti 2010). At the same time competition in the advertising market has accelerated with the entrance of a new commercial channel (Suomi-tv, part of the Canadian Astral Media Corporation). In early 2010, relations between the two biggest commercial companies (MTV3 and Sanoma Group) broke down in public, and MTV3 withdrew from the Finnish Television Association.

Charging for online content

Several Finnish newspapers have announced that they will start to charge for their online content. Most newspapers have already slimmed down their online news provision. *Keskisuomalainen*, an influential regional daily newspaper, was the first to announce that from 1 January 2011 it will start charging for an online paper. Several other newspapers immediately said they will follow this example.

Reorganising editorial processes

One side of the industry responses has to do with the business strategies outlined above, another has to do with a reorganisation of the editorial process.

Improving newsroom efficiency

In several companies, a system of 'corporate editorial leadership' has been deployed, nominating a joint editor-in-chief for several smaller newspapers. In some newspapers, a joint journalistic and financial leadership has been established, which means that the editor-in-chief acts also as the managing director of the publishing company (*Helsingin Sanomat, Satakunnan Kansa, Etelä-Suomen Sanomat*). This has led to an awkward situation where the editor-in-chief tries to balance between professional journalistic aims and values and the commercial expectations of the owners. New systems of corporate editorial departments are developed, where a joint foreign news department serves several (eight altogether) regional newspapers (including *Turun Sanomat, Kaleva, Etelä-Suomen Sanomat, Väli-Suomen Media*).

Reorganisation of journalistic work

Experienced and specialised journalists are reassigned to work in 'teams', that is, to do routine desk jobs on non-specialised beats. Instead of well-prepared and investigated reports more emphasis is invested in 'blog'-type journalism, columns and opinions of individual journalists. Print journalists are assigned to do online shifts as part of their weekly routines. Visual effects are used to substitute for deeper analysis. Increasing haste brings about rising amounts of 'cut-and-paste' journalism, based on PR material with little or no journalistic input (Nieminen 2010).

Cutting editorial costs

Despite the absence of an imminent crisis, the reaction of most newspaper publishers to the decline in income has been quite harsh. The basic approach has been to cut editorial costs. In 2009, 197 journalists were laid off from Finnish newspapers. (The total number of journalists in Finland is about 15,000: Nieminen 2010). The National Union of Finnish Journalists held fifty-four legal consultations with the media companies concerning industrial disputes. YLE announced its intention to cut a total of 311 employees (out of 3,600) by the year 2012 and it is additionally considering closing down one television channel. *Turun Sanomat* (the second biggest regional daily) reduced its journalistic staff by a third in 2009. Instead of permanent staff, people are employed under 'work-on-demand' contracts. Another method is to terminate old freelance contracts and to sign up new, cheaper but also less experienced and often non-professional contributors.

Redefining journalistic content

Make content sell better

Facing a slow but steady decline in readership, the press has to do more to attract readers and advertisers. One answer is the tabloidisation of the contents. Two rival Finnish evening tabloid papers have been struggling with declining sales, although the number of their online readers has been multiplying. The general perception is that their fierce competition has led to increasing sensationalism and political populism. The quality papers too, plagued by declining circulation, have been accused of the same increased personalisation, intrusion on privacy, growing emphasis on crime, accidents, personal grievances (see Karppinen and Jääsaari 2007; Mediatoorumi 2009).

Bringing issues closer to the readers

Early experiences with citizen journalism have given way to more journalism-centred approaches on how to get readers to better engage with the content. Leading trends are *localism*, journalism that addresses the issues and problems close to the reader's neighbourhood, and *advocacy* or *service journalism*, which takes up topical social problems, close to readers' lives (Kunelius and Reunanen 2008).

Inviting readers' contributions

Several different means have been used to engage readers. One recent ploy has been the increasing hosting of user-generated content (UGC) – photos, email messages, text messages, chat rooms etc., although it is unclear what the longer term consequences will be – as the quality of UGC is mostly poor and its subject issues are seldom original, it is questionable how long it will remain attractive (Heinonen 2008).

Making news journalism 'look better' by modernising the layout

The media groups are simplifying and visualising the make-up patterns and procedures to simplify and economise in the editorial processes. In order to make the content interchangeable between each corporation's newspapers, modular design systems are used.

The responses of policy-makers

As explained above, the Finnish media long enjoyed the status of national institutions, supporting and supported by the consensual social contract. From the late 1980s, this situation started to change, and more conflictual social and political relations began to substitute for consensus. The Finnish media and communication policy has – as in most European countries – steadily moved from the national-democratic line towards the EU-led competition policy that is more favourable to commercial actors. In 2010 the altered status of the media can be observed especially in three sectors of media policy: broadcasting, the printed press, and broadband.

Redefining the remit of YLE

As a reaction to changes in the media environment and the pressure of commercial broadcasters, the centre-right government appointed a committee (the YLE Committee) early in 2008 to consider the public service provision and financing of YLE. Commercial companies claim that YLE has seriously exceeded its public service remit and is preventing commercial companies from benefiting from the expected advertising revenue. The composition of the committee was politically broadly based, with representatives from all parliamentary parties.

The YLE Committee published its report in February 2009. Following the Finnish consensual tradition, the committee was unanimous in its result. Its main recommendations were moderate and concentrated mostly on details. In reference to the financing of YLE, the committee recommended a 'Public Service Media fee' to be collected from 'all household dwelling units'. In order to improve the monitoring of YLE public service obligations, the role of the Administrative Council was to be strengthened and clarified. The committee did not recommend any changes in YLE's administrative structure. It concluded that the present structure was well suited to the challenges of the changing media (LVM 2009).

The reaction of the Federation of the Finnish Media Industry was unexpectedly critical. It issued a statement in June 2009 claiming, among other things, that (Finnish Media Industry 2009):

- YLE's public service remit is not defined precisely enough in the report to facilitate its necessary measurement.

- The report does not propose the necessary restrictions on YLE's presence in the online environment.

- The committee's proposals do not guarantee independent control of YLE's public service activities; this is why there is a need for an external body to assess YLE's public service operation.

- The proposed Public Service Media fee is not appropriate for YLE's financing, The best solution would be financing by direct taxation.

This prompted a long and difficult process of negotiation. Finally, in March 2010 Minister of Communications Ms Lindén announced that the whole reform would be postponed until after the next parliamentary elections in the spring of 2011.

Amidst this political game a new Director General for YLE was elected. It was generally assumed that the incumbent DG, Mr Mikael Jungner, would be re-elected. However, in February 2010 the YLE Board of Directors nominated an outsider with a strong industry background, Mr Lauri Kivinen, who spent much of his career working for Nokia. What his blueprint is for the future of YLE is yet to be seen.

Promotion of a broadband network

As a part of the Information Society Strategy, the government is actively promoting the construction of a national high-speed broadband network based on a fibre-optic trunk line. In the autumn of 2009 the government announced that Finland will be the first country in the world to introduce a Universal Service Obligation (USO) for broadband internet. By 1 July 2010 all Finnish households must be offered a broadband connection with a minimum speed of 1 Mbit/s. It is planned that by 2015 the speed will be increased to 100 Mbit/s.

The motives behind the government's broadband policy are mixed. On one hand, broadband offers the ailing newspaper industry new potential for developing their online news services, based on novel 'cross-media' applications; on the other, broadband opens a way for the television industry to transfer television broadcasting to the internet (IPTV), which reduces costs and creates new business opportunities. As television moves to the internet, more radio frequencies are released for new and more profitable services. In this way, everybody wins: the newspaper industry will get better access to paying customers; the television industry will gain more interactivity; and the telecommunication industry will have more frequencies for new services.

State aid to the newspaper industry

Based on a public-interest argument, Finnish governments used to subsidise newspapers significantly by different means (Normo 1998). Since the mid 1990s, direct state aid has been drastically cut (see Table 5.4). At its final stage, the state aid was directed to the ailing party press in order to promote political pluralism. Even this minimal subsidy was, however, judged to be in violation of the EU State Aid directive and it was accordingly abolished in 2008.

Today two forms of public subsidy remain: for the newspapers published in minority languages (Swedish, Same), €0.5 million, and for cultural and opinion journals, €1 million in 2009 (shared by 150 journals).

More important are the indirect public subsidies, such as the zero tax rating of newspapers (0 per cent VAT, amounting to an estimated €207 million per year, see Parkkola 2010) and the reduced delivery charge for newspapers, making home delivery affordable for households in remote areas (amounting allegedly to more than €100 million per year) (GT-raportti 2010). The problem is that today both indirect forms of subsidy

Table 5.4. Government subsidies to newspapers 1989–2009

Year	1989	1992	1999	2003	2009
Euro (m)	43.91	37.36	12.60	12.60	0.50

Data: Statistics Finland 1995, 2010.

are jeopardised because of deregulatory pressures from the Ministry of Finance. If these subsidies were axed, it would result in great difficulties for the whole Finnish media structure. On behalf of the industry, the Ministry of Transport and Communication is investigating alternative ways to promote the same goals (LVM 2010).

Conclusions: democracy and journalism in Finland

From the viewpoint of democracy, these developments point to two further issues. The first concerns the way that the changes in journalism have been addressed in Finnish public debate; the second deals with more general challenges that Finnish democracy is facing today.

There has been relatively little open debate in Finland over the consequences of current media developments for democracy. A few public interventions took place in 2009 and early 2010, including a couple of public conferences and some critical debate (see Mediafoorumi 2009; RTTL 2009; Liiton Arkki 2010). The main issues in the debate have been the following.

The future of journalism

There is a widespread anxiety about the quality of journalism. Both the numbers of news journalists and the time available for creating a news story are in decline. It is feared that the decline in the resources for quality journalism may result in lowering the standard of serious, in-depth reporting.

The informational divide

There is growing concern about the divide between 'information rich' and 'information poor'. Growing costs in providing quality and investigative journalism have resulted in increases in the price of quality information. Traditional professional journalism becomes a privilege of the informed elite. The mass audience is left to consume 'free' information – advertising-funded free online services and free newspapers, which seldom offer original and well-researched journalistic content. As a result of the multiplication of entertainment television channels, public exposure to quality news programmes reduces.

Threats to democracy

There is a mounting fear that democratic and cultural values in media and communications policy are jeopardised. The policy planning and policy measures are increasingly justified on the basis of enhancing market competition, not of cultural and social goals. This market logic has penetrated all policy sectors: broadcasting policy, where PSB is restricted in order not to harm the market; telecommunications, where USO is interpreted for the benefit of the industry; and the public availability of newspapers, where EC stipulations are applied against the citizens' interests.

It must be finally emphasised, however, that the changes in the Finnish media system and journalism, described above, are closely related to more general societal and cultural trends and should be analysed in the context of these wider transformations in society. The long decline in newspaper circulation from the late 1980s has been accompanied by several simultaneous changes in Finnish society. A major period was in the early 1990s when Finland suffered from a deep economic recession, amounting to a drop of 10 per cent in GDP between 1991 and 1993. The recovery strategy by the government included a radical change not only in political style – from the long-prevailing consensual neo-corporatism towards a more antagonistic majoritarian style of politics – but also in basic governmental social and political philosophy (Julkunen 2001, 2006; Hänninen et al. 2010).

From the 1960s onwards, the Finnish national strategy was based on the Nordic model of social welfare ideology, aimed at promoting equality in all areas of social life (Bergholm 2007). Now the emphasis has changed: instead of social welfare, economic competitiveness and efficiency have been adopted as the main goals for national policies. This has contributed to drastic cuts in public spending in many areas, including social welfare, health care, old age pensions, education, etc. The consequences are becoming visible: between 1995 and 2005, the rise in income differences in Finland was the highest among all of the OECD countries, and the gap still continues to grow. Even the OECD warned Finland in 2008 of the expected – and today experienced – social and political costs of this trend (OECD 2010).

All this has obviously had consequences for the way in which citizens assess politics and politicians, with significant effects on the conditions and functions of the media too. Although public trust in institutions and authorities is still very high in Finland compared to many other European countries, confidence in politics and politicians has decreased sharply in recent years (Komu and Hellsten 2010; Grönlund 2010). This is reflected not only in domestic politics but also in the critical public attitude towards the EU. The level of distrust in politics can be illustrated by the trend in electoral participation. The main trend is a major drop in voting, both in national and local elections (from turnout around 80 per cent in the 1970s and 1980s to turnout below 70 per cent in the 2000s). The decrease has been most notable among young voters: in the age group of 18–24 years (male voters), voting activity decreased from 77 to 31 per cent between 1975–83 and 2007 (Om 2010).

An easy conclusion is that the results show that parliamentary democracy has not been able to deliver relative to citizen expectations. Why vote if you cannot expect any benefit from it? Many politicians, however, have put the blame on the media. The claim is that, because the media have turned more and more critical and even hostile to politics and politicians, they have contributed to civic cynicism and political passivity. In other words, the media and journalists have not been able to act as an efficient intermediary between the citizenry and political decision-makers, but are instead using their power for their own benefit (see e.g. Mediaviikko.fi 2008; EVA 2009b: 51).

It is against this general background that the developments in the Finnish media and journalism must be assessed. It can be argued that it is not so much a crisis of the media system and journalism as a wider rupture in the Finnish model of social contract. The sphere of national politics – traditionally the core subject area for journalism – has been drastically narrowed and redefined. As more and more public policies and public services are, due to privatisation and outsourcing, transferred to the market, the role and significance of national politics have become increasingly confused. This has also left the function of the media and journalism progressively more unclear. If we think that the role of the media and journalism should be to speak to the national audience, or national audiences, there are simply fewer and fewer substantial issues around which the national audience could be constructed today.

This does not mean, however, that there is no demand for professional journalism. As in most other countries in Europe, different forms of social activism and democratic participation are proliferating in Finland too, and there is certainly an increasing need felt for information and informed opinions. What is new, however, is that with the advent of the new ICT, and especially the internet, the modes of communication have drastically changed and the traditional media have been found wanting from the point of view of people's new communicative needs.

From this perspective, it is not primarily the challenge of the internet and the new digital technology that is changing the media and journalism landscape in Finland. It is more that the internet has been domesticated in a particular historical context. In the same way, we cannot say that it is the global financial crisis that is shaping the future of the Finnish media and journalism; rather the significance of the crisis is that it is accelerating developments which already have been ongoing for a long time.

References

Antikainen, H. O. Kuusisto, A. Bäck, O. Nurmi and A. Viljakainen (2010) *Viestintäalan nykytila ja kehitystrendit 2010-2011*. GT-raportti. Nro 1, maaliskuu 2010. VTT:n mediatekniikan asiantuntijapalvelu. Helsinki: VTT.

Bergholm, T. (2007) 'Suomen mallin synty'. *Yhteiskuntapolitiikka*, 72/5: 475–92.

EVA (2009a) 'EVA Report "In Search of Modern Times" is published' (25 Nov.): www.eva.fi/eng/index.php?m=2&show=423 (accessed March 2010).

— (2009b) *Kapitalismi kansan käräjillä: EVAn kansallinen arvo- ja asennetutkimus 2009*. Helsinki: EVA, www.eva.fi/wp-content/uploads/files/2416_kapitalismi_kansan_karajilla.pdf (accessed July 2010).

Finnish Media Industry (2009) 'Lausunto Yleisradio Oy:n julkista palvelua ja rahoitusta selvittävän työryhmän ehdotuksista. Viestinnän keskusliitto r.y', in *Lausuntokokoelma: Yleisradio Oy:n julkista palvelua ja rahoitusta selvittävän työryhmän ehdotukset*, pp. 80–90 (25 June): www.lvm.fi/c/document_library/get_file?folderId=597411&name=DLFE-8047.pdf&title (accessed March 2010).

Finnpanel.fi (2010) 'Results from the TV Audience Measurement': www.finnpanel.fi/en/tulokset/tv.php (accessed April 2010).

Grönlund, K. (2010) 'Demokratian tila Suomessa', *MTV3:n ja Oikeusministeriön Talviareena-seminaari*, Eduskunta 10 Feb.

Hänninen, S., E. Palola, and M. Kaivonurmi, eds (2010) *Mikä meitä jakaa? Hyvinvointipolitiikkaa kilpailuvaltiossa*. Helsinki: THL.

Harcourt, A. (2005) *The European Union and the Regulation of Media Markets*. Manchester and New York: Manchester University Press.

Heinonen, A. (2008). *Yleisön sanansijat sanomalehdissä*. Tiedotusopin laitos, Journalismin tutkimusyksikkö. Julkaisuja A108. Tampere: Tampereen yliopisto.

Herkman, J. (2009) 'The Democratic Corporatist Model: The Case of Finland', *Javnost: The Public*, 16/4: 73–90.

Julkunen, R. (2001) *Suunnanmuutos: 1990-luvun sosiaalipoliittinen reformi Suomessa*. Tampere: Vastapaino.

— (2006) *Kuka vastaa? Hyvinvointivaltion rajat ja julkinen vastuu*. Helsinki: Stakes.

Karppinen, K. and J. Jääsaari (2007) *Suomalaisten käsityksiä mediasta ja vallasta*. *Raportti kyselytutkimuksesta*: www.hssaatio.fi/pdf/SurveyValta.pdf (accessed March 2010).

Komu, M. and K. Hellsten (2010) *Luottamus ihmisiin ja luottamus instituutioihin Euroopassa.* Nettityöpapereita 12/2010. Kelan tutkimusosasto. Helsinki: Kela/Fpa.

Kunelius, R. and E. Reunanen (2008) 'Iltalehden suuri lupaus: Osallistuva journalismi ja populismin karikot', *Journalismikritiikin vuosikirja, Tiedotustutkimus,* 31/2: 45–56.

Liiton, A. (2010) 'Tutkiva journalismi tuottaa parempia tuloksia', *Liiton Arkki* 1/2010: www.rttl.fi/fi/index.php/liiton_arkki/38/801 (accessed May 2010).

LVM (2009) *Public Service and Funding of the Finnish Broadcasting Company YLE. Final Working Group Report.*

— (2010) *Postilakiehdotus ja lehtijakelu: Selvitysmiehen väliraportti,* Liikenne- ja viestintäministeriö, 16 March 2010, www.lvm.fi/c/document_library/get_file?f olderId=964902&name=DLFE-10645.pdf&title=Postilakiehdotus ja lehtijakelu. Selvitysmiehen väliraportti (accessed July 2010).

Mainostajat.fi (2010) 'Mediamainonnan määrä laski voimakkaasti vuonna 2009', Finnish Advertising Council/Mainonnan neuvottelukunta, press release 28 Jan.: www.mainostajat.fi/mliitto/sivut/Mainosvuosi2010lehdistotiedote.pdf (accessed April 2010).

Markkinointi ja mainonta (2010) 'Takatalvi iski mediamainontaan', *Markkinointi ja mainonta,* 21 May: www.marmai.fi/uutiset/article407806. ece?s=l&wtm=Markkinointi_Mainonta/-21052010 (accessed July 2010).

Mediafoorumi (2009) *Voidaanko journalismin yhteiskunnallinen tehtävä pelastaa?* TAT: Helsinki.

Mediaviikko.fi (2008) 'Selvitys: Kansan mielestä median valta kasvaa', *Mediaviikko* (18 Jan.): http://mediaviikko.fi/kaikki/uutinen/selvitys-kansan-mielesta-median-valta-kasvaa.html (accessed July 2010).

Michalis, M. (2007) *Governing European Communication: From Unification to Coordination.* Plymouth: Lexington Books.

Nieminen, A. (2010) An interview with Mr. Arto Nieminen, President of the National Union of Journalists, 28 Jan.

Normo, E. (1998) 'Sanomalehdistön tukeminen Pohjoismaissa', *Joukkoviestimet: Finnish Mass Media 1998.* Helsinki: Tilastokeskus – Statistics Finland, 39–57.

OECD 2010: *Economic Survey of Finland, 2010.* Policy Brief, April: www.oecd.org/ dataoecd/48/9/44897180.pdf (accessed July 2010).

Om (2010) *Nuorten ääni – aikuisten uurna?* Äänioikeusikärajatyöryhmän raportti, Oikeisministeriön julkaisuja 49/2010, www.om.fi/1274105479546 (accessed June 2010).

Parkkola, T. (2010) Arvonlisäverotukseen liittyviä erityiskysymyksiä, 9 Feb.: www.vm.fi/ vm/fi/05_hankkeet/012_veroryhma/06_esitysaineisto/ALV-erityiskysymyksia_ Parkkola_09022010_esitys.pdf (accessed April 2010).

RTTL (2009) 'Kuka pelastaisi journalismin? Mediaseminaari 15.10.': www.rttl.fi/fi/ upload/files/mediaseminaari.ohjelma.pdf (accessed May 2010).

van Cuilenburg, J., and D. McQuail (2003) 'Media Policy Paradigm Shifts: Towards a New Communications Policy Paradigm', *European Journal of Communication,* 18/2: 181–207.

6. The French Press and its Enduring Institutional Crisis

Alice Antheaume

Translated by Cécile Dehesdin

Introduction

The crisis in the French press is nothing new. It is rooted in a model created sixty years ago, at the end of the Second World War. Designed for the post-war environment, that model has been showing its limits for several years now. It should have been reformed several times, in the 1970s, the 1980s, or the 1990s. There have been several attempts to do so, either because individual newspapers were going through a rough time or because the industry as such could no longer function. They came to nothing. The failure to find long-term solutions has led to a growth in direct state aid to the press, together with a more general expansion of government involvement with the newspaper industry.

Today, the French print media are thrashing about between reliance on state subsidies and a desire for independence. When the digital revolution and then the financial crisis came, neither the national dailies nor the regional papers were ready. The shock was so violent that, once more, the French government intervened, this time creating the États Généraux de la Presse Écrite – the Round Table of Print Media – and unrolling new subsidies.

The origins of the current French newspaper model

Before the Second World War, the relationship between large industrial magnates and the press seemed stronger in France than in other Western countries. Organised through the 'Comité des Forges' – the major iron and steel owners' organisation – large manufacturing companies owned newspapers and used them to defend their own interests and dominate the areas in which they operated. This relationship took on a strong political dimension during moments of crisis and political polarisation, such as during the period of the Popular Front in 1936, when parts of the French press engaged in a ferocious campaign against Léon Blum and his left-wing government.

During the Second World War, some print outlets – including their printing houses and distributors – collaborated with the Vichy government and Nazi Germany, while another type of print media emerged, created in underground networks and spreading the Résistance's ideals.

The end of the Second World War came with a bitter reality: the traditional press was seen as corrupt, in the pocket of big business and tainted by collaboration. In 1945, General de Gaulle's provisional government, which included people from all the different political groups that had participated in the Résistance, decided on an overhaul of the French press based around Résistance ideals.

They 'purged' the so-called 'collaborationist' press. The purge affected both organisations (press companies, printing houses, and distribution companies) and people (reporters and newspaper owners). All newspapers and weeklies that had started after 25 June 25 1940 (the date of the Franco-German armistice) were closed under the ordinance of 30 September 1944. Collaborationists lost their offices and their means of distribution. Journalists who had for example received a promotion during the German occupation or worked for an outlet that had been deemed to be strategically important for Germany were suspended for two years in 90 per cent of cases by the Commission de la carte d'identité professionnelle des journalistes français, the official organ in charge of handing out press cards in France. This committee proceeded to suspend 687 journalists out of the 8,200 files it went through in 1945 and 1946 (according to the press historian Patrick Eveno (2008)).

Among the ideals of the Résistance was the idea that the state should have a protective role and organise and ensure media pluralism: for many of the political groups that fought with the Résistance, a reliance on the market was seen as a route to inevitable concentration of ownership, and something that would prevent the full range of political viewpoints from being expressed.

This explains why under the immediate post-war arrangements it was the Minister of Information (a position that no longer exists) who had to grant newspapers authorisation to publish, and even decided the price at which they should be sold. Starting in 1944, *L'Humanité*, *Le Figaro* and *La Croix*, to take only newspapers that still exist in 2010, got the authorisation to be issued or to be issued again. On 28 February 1946, the first issue of the sports daily *L'Equipe* came out – it remains the highest circulation daily in 2010. Meanwhile, the underground papers launched by the Résistance fighters during the war found their place in the post-war French press environment. *La Voix du Nord*, *Nord Eclair*, *France Soir* (created from the resistance paper *Défense de la France*), and *Le Monde*, which was set up in the former offices of the newspaper *Le Temps*.

However, all these papers still needed to address the lack of means to print and distribute newspapers during the shortages of the immediate post-war years. The idea emerged of pooling resources through a system of co-operatives. On the production side, the CGT book printing union now controlled all the printworks and had to be relied on to print newspapers. On the distribution side, new co-operatives were created. After the expropriation of the Messageries Hachette in the aftermath of the liberation, the Nouvelles Messageries de la Presse Parisienne (NMPP) – today called Presstalis – was born. This organisation was granted a monopoly over distribution and five publishing co-operatives jointly owned 51 per cent of its capital. Its power was astounding: it was and still is almost the only organisation distributing national dailies and magazines in France.

Another idea from the Résistance was to exclude big business and industry magnates from owning and funding the French press, or to put it simply, to avoid the creation of new oligopolistic groups and the return of the power of employers groups such as the Comité des Forges. It was a way of forbidding the 'finance world from taking over newspapers', to quote the *Journal Officiel* from February 1947.

The model's weakness

From the beginning, the system devised suffered from structural difficulties and contextual constraints: the price of paper increased, printing plants experienced various management problems, the printers' trade union called numerous strikes and, above all, the readers were losing interest. According to the numbers put together by Fabrice D'Almeida and Christian Delporte (2003), France went from 203 dailies in 1946 to 123 in 1958. Similarly circulation declined, from 15.1 million in 1946 to 11.6 million in 1958.

It wasn't obvious at the time but in the background, the crisis among the readers was already developing. 'Everybody wants to write, each party wants its paper, we're explaining, analyzing, describing, justifying, we're trying to take the French people higher and higher, to finally turn this cattle into lions. The problem is, French people don't want to hear any of it', commented the then editor-in-chief of the daily *France Soir*, Charles Baudinat (quoted in Eveno 2008).

The situation was becoming unsustainable, and the state decided to intervene to try to rescue the press. It started by giving out emergency aid, both directly through subsidies and grants to buy equipment, and indirectly by helping circulation through reduced postage and transport costs or by reducing VAT. From now on, the state would have to foot more and more of an increasing bill.

In 2010, sixty years after those mechanisms were created, the post-war corporatist system of management is still in place in the French press. The printing works are still controlled by the CGT print union and Presstalis (the former NMPP) is still in charge of distribution. Today it still supplies more than 29,000 retail outlets in France. Though it is more and more called into question, this system of equal representation of both industry and co-operatives within each firm (called 'paritarisme') is still in effect.

In 1983, the anti-concentration principle was reflected in a new law specifying that a single player could not own several dailies if their combined circulation exceeded 15 per cent of the market. Another law, passed on 30 September 1986, restated the objective of avoiding a limited number of media owners. All of which conflicted with the objective of creating national 'French champions' in the sector. Despite this law, or maybe because of it, the presence of major industrial players from outside the sector has been growing in French media. The building company Bouygues bought the TV channel TF1 in 1987; the Aeronautics giant Dassault has owned the daily *Le Figaro* since 2004. Finally, the economics daily paper *Les Echos* has been owned by the luxury goods group LVMH since 2007.

The French model for newspapers has in recent years been experiencing an increasingly acute crisis which has been causing more and more alarm. The co-operative model, designed for times of shortage, is ill equipped to deal with an abundance of media. The 'closed shop' union system that dominates daily newspaper printing plants leads to far higher production costs in France than abroad. Those costs are passed on to the consumers, who consequently buy fewer newspapers because they are too expensive. Not only do most readers not buy different dailies on a given day, but they do not buy the same daily every day either. (Meanwhile the French buy comparatively many more news-magazines, which benefit from lower production costs.) Newspaper readership in France has decreased from 250 to 167 copies sold per 1,000 residents between 1950 and 2000, whereas in the same period readership increased in Germany (from 300 to 322) and Italy (from 120 to 158) (figures form Eveno 2008).

Between 1965 and 1995, the French press has been the most expensive press in the world to produce. For example, in 2008 printing 30,000 copies of a 22-page *International Herald Tribune* cost €3854 in France, €2334 in England, €1661 in Germany, and €2229 in Italy (États Généraux de la Presse Écrite 2009).

For that reason, few new dailies are created in France. Between 1970 and 2010, leaving aside free sheets, the only dailies that launched were *Libération* (1973), *Le Quotidien de Paris* (1974), *Le Matin de Paris* (1977), *La Tribune* (1985), *Le Sport* (1987), and *InfoMatin* (1994). In 2010, only *Libération* and *La Tribune* survived, the former saved in 2007 thanks to the state and Edouard de Rotschild's financial support; the latter sold in 2010 for €1 by Alain Weill, president of the media group NextRadioTV, to its CEO Valérie Decamp.

Faced with globalisation, French anti-concentration laws mean that the country's press cannot rely on big media conglomerates for support. Likewise, no print group in France can be present on all platforms – the law allows a group to own several TV channels, several national radio stations and several national dailies only if those dailies do not exceed a 20 per cent circulation threshold across the country. This results in a relative undercapitalisation and sometimes in a need for financing by industrialists and funders outside of the media world, some of whom rely on state contracts.

The rise of the internet, the financial crisis, and their impact on the French media system

Like the rest of the world, the French press is undergoing a digital tsunami. But one should not forget that print media were the first media organisations to go online, before TV or radio. From 1995 to about 2007, print media dominated online information in France. Their websites saw an exponential growth of visitors. *Le Monde*'s website, Lemonde.fr, went from 20,000 visits a day in 1998 to 100,000 in 2001, then over a million at the end of 2006, reaching a million and a half in 2010 (see Patino in *La Tribune* 2010).

The spread of high-speed internet access from 2003 onwards did not put an immediate end to print media's dominance of online news. The number of visitors has kept growing as video and to some extent sound became regular features of print

Table 6.1. Total unique visitors, top news websites, March 2010

Lemonde.fr (newspaper)	6,993,000
Lefigaro.fr (newspaper)	4,100,000
20minutes.fr (freesheet)	3,397,000
TF1 news (broadcaster)	2,294,000
Liberation.fr (newspaper)	1,747,000

Data from Comscore, March 2010

outlets' websites, which have also started to welcome blogs, audience participation and other user-generated content (La Tribune 2010). (See Table 6.1.)

However, the end of the first decade of the twenty-first century saw a relative slump of print outlets' websites, as three types of competitors emerged: portals and search engines, whose aggregating power, often automatic, overshadows any individual press outlet's reach (Google News and Yahoo! News); the online only 'pure players', whose specialisation or capacity for innovation gives them an advantage (Rue89, Médiapart); and finally, broadcast outlets, with an emphasis on video production (e.g. TF1 News). Print now has to fight to stay on top, and digital does not seem to be the only solution to the continuing crisis in the industry anymore. The old model will not be saved through a natural mutation towards the new one. The journey will be more complicated.

While the erosion of readership used to be a very slow phenomenon that started decades ago in France, the decline has accelerated dramatically in a matter of a few years. Digital technologies have caused a more rapid fragmentation of media consumption since the audience divides a fixed amount of time between several platforms (print, computer screens, TV/radio and, growing in a spectacular manner, mobile phones).

On top of this phenomenon, another trend is polarising each platform internally: those who used to read several newspapers tend to read less of them to keep more time for their new habits (the same goes for the number of TV channels watched, with the viewers tending to close up on a share that's proportionally narrower than the growing offer of channels). Fragmentation and polarisation do not put an end to the use of print, but they reduce its consumption. The disappearance of its readers does not equal a death sentence for print media, but it does threaten them by weakening their business model: media diets are diversifying to the point where economic models are feeding off – and slowly killing – each other.

Today, the old business model is dying faster than new ones are being built: if in France print media's websites have quickly reached a sometimes spectacular mass audience success, their economic weight remains disappointing. Print media's digital revenues never compensated for the decrease in 'traditional' revenue. The same goes for digital profits – where there are any. At the beginning of the second decade of the twenty-first

Figure 6.1. Evolution of total newspaper revenues (1990–2008)

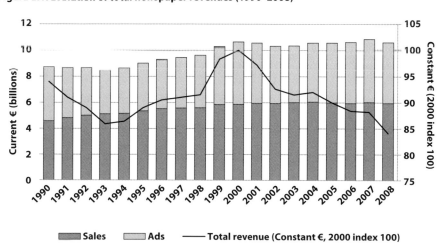

Sales   Ads   —— Total revenue (Constant €, 2000 index 100)

Data from DDM (2009).

century, online information is still in search of a business model: a free website model became the rule between 1996 and 2008 with the intention of riding the wave of the spectacular increase in advertising, but the revenues quickly appeared to be insufficient, hence the beginning of mixed models (Lemonde.fr since 2002) and often difficult attempts to establish pay walls and rely on subscription revenue (La Tribune 2010).

To these structural changes, one must add a difficult conjuncture. Advertising revenues had already suffered during the dot.com bubble in 2000, and have been enduring the consequences of the financial crisis since 2008. As print media advertising revenues decline faster than their online counterparts increase, the relative size of national print media is reduced: the total revenue of national dailies was, in 2008, at its lowest since 1990, because of a continuous fall in revenues from advertising, classifieds in particular. In 1990, national dailies and news-magazines amounted for 19.3 per cent of all press advertising, compared to 14.2 per cent in 2008 (Direction du développement des médias 2009).

Moreover, dailies' circulation numbers have been decreasing. *Le Figaro* went from a circulation of 332,863 copies in 2006 to 314,947 copies in 2009 ; *Le Monde* from 350,039 in 2006 to 288,049 in 2009; even *L'Equipe*, France's most sold daily, went from 365,411 in 2006 to 303,305 in 2009. At the same time, since 2005, several daily freesheets have been created in France, where there is a distinction between information freesheets (which include editorial content) and classified ads freesheets (with little or no editorial content). In 2010, the best known information freesheets are *20 Minutes*, *Metro*, and *Direct Matin*. *20 Minutes*, for instance, has been conceived by a reporter from *Libération*, Frédéric Filloux, and has hired many journalists from the traditional press. It's name reflects the idea that it takes about 20 minutes to read the whole newspaper, usually in the subway or in the bus (freesheets are, as elsewhere, present only in big cities). The circulation of *20 Minutes* was about 709,000 copies in 2009 (figures from Association pour le contrôle de la diffusion des médias, OJD), and freesheets account for a growing share of total newspaper circulation in France.

The crisis has not only been affecting national dailies. Regional newspapers, which for a long time constituted an economic exception to the general pattern in France,

Figure 6.2. Daily national general-interest newspapers, revenue (1990–2008)

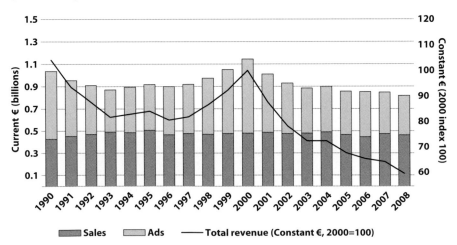

Sales ▢ Ads —— Total revenue (Constant €, 2000=100)

Data from DDM (2009).

have been suffering a sudden decline in classified ads, their main source of revenue, since 2009. Magazines were always very successful in France and for a long time sheltered from the crisis, but their circulation has recently been going down too (-4.8 per cent in 2008; -4.5 per cent in 2009), as have their advertising revenues (-4.7 per cent in 2008) (Direction du développement des médias 2009).

However the end of the financial crisis will not be enough to resolve the French print media's issues, because its weakness comes first and foremost from its outdated business model. Newspapers' costs are too high, especially production costs. The printing of a daily in France constitutes between 20 and 35 per cent of its overall costs. A task group at the États Généraux de la Presse Écrite (2009), the official round table of print media, concluded that this was in part due to the wage costs of printing plants, which are often overstaffed and where the workers are overpaid.

The consequences for newsrooms

Operating in an outmoded institutional framework and caught between the economic crisis and the digital revolution, French newsrooms are suffering today. Undercapitalised since 1945, media groups cannot handle these shocks or set in motion the measures needed to secure future profitability. National and regional newspapers are losing money, sometimes up to 10 per cent of their revenues, and they are often desperately looking for investors.

For example, the Sud Ouest group, the third largest regional newspaper company in France, is in financial trouble. In 2007 it bought for €90 million several newspapers in the South of France (*Midi Libre*, *L'Indépendant* and *Centre Presse*) and acquired a classified ads publisher for €50 million. It was supposed to team up with another paper, *La Dépêche du Midi*, to buy these companies. But *La Dépêche* changed its mind at the last minute, and Sud Ouest had to buy them on its own.

Hersant Media, owner of the regional paper *Nice Matin*, is crippled with debts. *Nice Matin* is for sale, its employees have gone on strike several times, and the paper's president, Eric Debry, resigned in April 2010. Beyond anecdotal evidence, it is hard to draw an overall picture of the impact the digital revolution and financial crisis had on French newsrooms, because no official numbers exist. But a few indicators allow us to take stock of its scale.

The number of press passes allocated in 2009 is down from the year before, for the first time since 1935 when the French press passes were created as an identity card of sorts for professional journalists (it also gives them tax breaks). In 2008, 37,307 press passes were granted (20,945 for men, 16,362 for women).

Another sign of job insecurity is that the proportion of professional journalists without a full-time contract has reached 20 per cent. Layoffs and more or less voluntary redundancies in newspapers like *Le Figaro*, *Le Parisien*, *Prisma Presse* or *Sud Ouest* are adding up. *Le Monde* let 20 per cent of its newsroom go in 2008 and is getting ready for another wave of people leaving in 2010 during its recapitalisation. The media group L'Express Roularta let 10 per cent of its newsroom go, and *Libération* has also faced two waves of cost cutting. In the end, journalists have few opportunities to be hired in print newsrooms today. The only newsrooms able to offer long-term contracts to young reporters are web-based, like lexpress.fr, 20minutes.fr, lefigaro.fr, and a few 'pure players'. To try and survive, print media needs to reinvent itself: reinvent its production model, its operating model, and adapt to the new technological situation.

Figure 6.3. Press passes issued in France

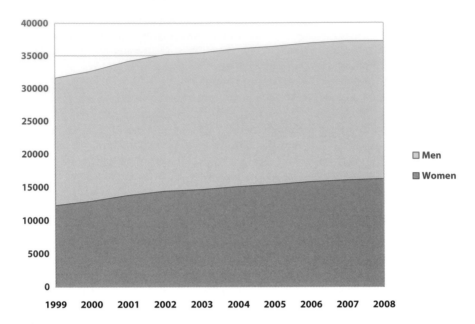

The total number of French press cards issued every year. In light grey, press cards issued to men. In dark grey, press cards issued women. Data from the French Commission de la carte d'identité des journalistes professionnels.

Reactions from the Sarkozy government

The generalised crisis of print media brought on, as often in France, state intervention. French president Nicolas Sarkozy launched the États Généraux de la Presse Écrite, a national consultation process, with every organisation, union, and printer who wanted to be heard, between 2008 and 2009. Four task groups were given four missions: the first considered 'the future of journalism jobs', directed by Bruno Frappat, CEO of group Bayard Presse; the second 'print, transport, distribution, funding: how to regenerate the industrial process of print media', directed by François Dufour, editor of a daily newspaper for children and the French representative at the World Association of Newspapers; the third 'the internet shock: what models for print media?', directed by Bruno Patino, the former president of Le Monde Interactif, now director of the public station France Culture (and also dean of the Journalism School of Sciences Po); and the fourth 'print media and society', directed by Arnaud de Puyfontaine, the former CEO of Emap France and Mondadori France.

'This extremely difficult situation calls for a personal obligation on everyone's part to preserve one of our democracy's most precious goods: independent, transparent and pluralistic print media outlets', the introduction to the report written as a conclusion to the round table reads, 'that's the cause that all participants to the round tables rallied around'. The report aims to be radical: 'in every country other than France, these circumstances brought the markets and its main players to drastic adaptations. It is in part going differently here: Standing squarely on its good intentions and its bad habits, partly sheltered by the protective cocoon of state support, the press is adjusting only marginally, seeing its antiquated practices as inevitable and surviving with difficulty.'

The French state justifies its commitment in several ways: the President wants to 'act' and 'shake up the story of a predicted decline'; one should not 'abandon print media to the laws of the market' and, more importantly, because the press encapsulates democratic virtues in its watchdog function (Etats Généraux de la Presse Écrite 2009).

This statement from the report drives home the message: 'The print media's health being one of the surest signs of a country's democratic vitality, it is legitimate that the authorities pursue a pro-active action to change a situation that ranks us among the weakest readers of dailies in developed countries.' So does the reference to those words by Jacques-Pierre Brissot, founder of newspaper the *Patriote* in 1789: 'A free gazette is like a sentinel constantly watching over society.' The state's intervention occurs in a very particular situation. French print media are already amongst the most subsidised in the world: public support represents about 8 per cent of the press's total revenue (États Généraux de la Presse Écrite 2009).

Nicolas Sarkozy and his government know the issue is tricky. 'the executive power would obviously be criticised if it ventured in the editorial or the ethical fields, which belong to editors and reporters'. The president wants to limit his action to three fields: 'understanding', through ten weeks of debate; 'reform', an idea dear to his heart; and 'anticipating' by 'encourag[ing] action'.

Here are the recommendations from each task group from the États Généraux (2009):

The future of journalism jobs

This group wants to promote a detailed ethical code, valid for all French professional reporters, and to reform the copyright system for journalists. Currently, most print journalists' contracts do not specify that their articles can be used on platforms other than print, like mobile phones, websites, etc., which constitutes one more difficulty when print groups try to develop their brand across multiple platforms. The group also felt newsrooms' heads should have direct contact with the audience, rather than nominating mediators supposed to help the newsroom and the audience connect.

Printing, transport, distribution and funding: how to regenerate the industrial process of print media

This group suggests that employment contracts at printing facilities be reformed to allow them to 'function at a reasonable cost', and employees be trained in new production techniques or new types of employment, through a 'long-term training plan'. Most of all, this task group proposed that newsstand sales be simplified, calling into question the Presstalis distribution system: the roundtable's report asks for more retail outlets 'by making the distributor's job more attractive', and by allowing publishers to distribute papers outside of the Presstalis co-operative system. Conscious of how difficult those changes would be to roll out, the task group proposed creating a 'Council for the retail sales of newspapers' which could negotiate the reform. It also suggested lowering subscription charges, to increase home deliveries, and to 'redistribute some of the state's advertising expenditures towards print media'. Finally, it reached an agreement with the Postal Service to lower postal costs for newspaper delivery for a year.

The internet shock: what models for print media?

This group recommends a fiscal policy aimed at encouraging the publishers of print media's websites to innovate, through tax breaks for individuals investing in these, and the creation of a 'digital publisher' legal status, which would open up a route to public support. Moreover, it advises to 'guarantee pluralism by making it compulsory, in a legal manner, for internet providers and search engines to be neutral by forbidding any discrimination based on the origins and the nature of content coming from publishers', as well as 'accelerate the set up of digital distribution of contents (ebooks, etc.) to get rid of the restraints of physical distribution'.

Print media and society

This group proposed that a free subscription to a daily newspaper of their choice should be offered to every young person at the age of 18 (750,000 people). The publisher and the state would share the cost 50/50. Other recommendations listed included creating the function of a 'journalist ambassador of under 25-year-old youth' inside newsrooms, who would be in charge of 'suggesting stories and pitches directed towards the youth during editorial meetings', as well as recognising 'the right for students to read dailies and magazines at school, including in study rooms'.

When the roundtables reached its conclusion, the government's share of the bill amounted to €600 million (€200 million a year for three years) to bring the print media industrial model back to life, including €20 million for the innovation policy proposed by the task group focusing on 'The internet shock: what models for print media?' This is both a lot and not enough money. It will not be enough to make up for the financial needs of the French print media. It may even be inadequate to meet the financial needs of print media in the next two years. But the government warnings were clear: the roundtable was to be the state's 'last effort'.

Despite those ten weeks of debate, the fundamental causes of the print crisis remain unresolved. The production and distribution system remain untouched. Closed shops still exist in printing works, along with editors' co-operatives. The future of Presstalis, which holds 80 per cent of the distribution market, has nonetheless been called into question. The government has made a treasury official, Inspecteur des finances Bruno Mettling, responsible for fundamentally rethinking the sixty-year-old French system of distribution.

Some of the main measures from the roundtable look very similar to other measures proposed in official reports fifteen years ago, in 1995, when Nicolas Sarkozy – then a minister under President Jacque Chirac – organised four committees to save the print industry. For example, home delivery was already then receiving €8 million in state subsidies. While some American newspapers are considering abandoning this system, the French government plans to give home delivery €70 million in subsidies – a disproportionate number when one knows that home delivery only represents 24 per cent of newspaper and magazines circulation in France in 2009.

Is this approach a French cultural characteristic? Perhaps. At least the death of a newspaper appears to be unthinkable for politicians in France.

Reactions from publishers

On the publishers' side, the answer seems to lie more in retrenching to defensive positions rather than in a forward-looking reform movement. The public offensive set out against Google, which has become one of the foremost advertising outlets in the world, is part of this counter-attack: publishers want to be paid because they consider they are the ones who provide some of the content indexed by the search engine, in particular for Google News. According to data from the media research company Outsell, 44 per cent of Google News visitors only read the articles' titles without clicking, hence not driving any traffic back to the site providing those articles. While 85 per cent of French people's online sessions include the use of a search engine, publishers want a piece of that cake, either directly (through royalties), or indirectly (by receiving part or all of the advertising revenues). Comparing Google's ads revenue (about €900 million in 2009), to Le Monde's (about €42 million) and to Lemonde.fr's (€14 million), one can see the gap is huge, another reason why Google scares publishers.

In addition to Google, the real-time web is another phenomenon worrying publishers. Competition is fierce in breaking news, especially between web newsrooms. But Agence France Presse (AFP, the French news agency) has been neglecting breaking news even though it is part of its supposed core mission. The AFP is not as competitive as it used to be and sometimes gets beaten by web newsrooms. AFP leaders are aware of the problem but have been redefining the agency's purpose, saying it no longer necessarily needs to be first to get the news out but needs to be the one to get reliable and relevant information out.

Likewise, print newsrooms are reluctant to publish their information and news scoops on their websites, often preferring to hold them back for the next day's printed edition. Newspaper managers often organise the copy flow around the print newsroom, instead of going full force on the web, seen as the source for all the print media's troubles.

Finally, one question remains unsolved for publishers: what business model should they go for online? Free? Pay walls? Freemium? Several news websites tried to determine what content they could make people pay for: Lefigaro.fr is testing out a mixed model, Liberation.fr makes people pay for any content from the print version of the paper, and Lemonde.fr started doing the latter too. But for now none of these methods has proved economically successful.

Conclusion

French print media is going through a situation not seen since the liberation at the end of the Second World War. Le Monde is being recapitalised by the threesome Pierre Bergé, Matthieu Pigasse, Xavier Niel (between 80 and 100 million euros); Le Parisien and La Tribune, two other national dailies, are up for sale. The inherited industrial nature of their model explains why newspapers are more affected by this evolution: their business model is based on the economies of scale of mass circulation product, the only thing able to repay the high production and distribution costs of a transient product. But when the trend moves in the opposite direction, it creates a vicious circle: the average cost increases, sometimes dramatically, while the revenues per copy decline the more advertising revenues plummet.

In France, journalism schools are thinking about changing their curriculum to adapt to these latest evolutions. Sciences Po Journalism School has decided to take the plunge: students have to be familiar with all the platforms (TV, radio, print, web) and all take digital journalism as a major subject, even those who do not aspire to become online journalists. Today newsrooms, whatever platform they produce to, want to recruit young reporters who know about all the functionalities of Google, know how to search for very precise data on the web, how to find them in real time, and how to produce content on social networks.

In the long run, one has to question the future funding of professionally produced news. In numerous Western countries, dailies are the keystone of the news circuit: they fund reporting and foreign desks and are the main clients (hence the main funding source) for news agencies, with broadcast media only contributing in a limited manner. The print model's very grave crisis translates into the impoverished funding for professional news collecting: foreign desks are closing, in-the-field reporting is becoming less frequent, contracts with news agencies are called into question. Still, online news does not, for now, offer an alternative financial model. 'Pure players' have developed their professional know-how, the best of them are now recognised as credible as newspapers' or print media's websites, but their financial firepower remains minimal, which means they cannot yet replace newspapers in the macro funding of professional news production.

The true debate is only just emerging: how can we save professional journalism (which isn't the same as saving one's monopoly as a content producer)? Some French intellectuals, like Collège de France historian Pierre Rosenvallon, and renowned journalists, are trying to promote the idea that information is a public good. In a lecture on public freedom as a democratic issue, Rosanvallon has argued that governments have to undergo 'validation tests' – which are different from elections – to be perfectly democratic. In his view, the state has to support and cultivate plural expression of the common good. Rosanvallon argues that 'information and the press, as far as it represents plural and different expressions, is part of the social contract' – not simply the social contract that we vote on when we have elections, but the underlying one that makes democracy possible.

References

Association pour le Le Controle des Diffusion des Medias (OJD) Commission de la carte d'identité des journalistes professionnels.

d'Almeida, F., and C. Delporte (2003) *Histoire des médias en France: De la Grande Guerre à nos jours*. Paris: Flammarion.

Direction du développement des médias (DDM) (2009) *La Presse écrite en 2008* (Info-MédiaS 15). Paris: Ministry of Culture and Communication: www.ddm.gouv.fr/IMG/pdf/infomedias_n15.pdf

États Généraux de la Presse Écrite (2009). *Livre vert*. Paris: Ministry of Culture and Communication: www.etatsgenerauxdelapresseecrite.fr/download/?lang=fr&mode=lenjeu&lenjeu_id=58

Eveno, P. (2008) *La Presse quotidienne nationale: Fin de partie ou renouveau?* Paris: Vuibert.

La Tribune, ed (2010) *Dictionnaire politique d'Internet et du numérique*. Paris: La Tribune.

7. The Press We Destroy

John Lloyd

Introduction

The British news media continue to present an image of relatively robust health. It is, however, an image which is increasingly hard to maintain, and which is being progressively hollowed out, at least in its still dominant mainstream of newspapers and broadcasters.

The country's newspapers remain powerful engines of opinion, scandal and news – at the national level. The columnists of both the upmarket and the popular press are taken seriously by the political class, by the politically engaged, and of course themselves: as yet, no large figure has emerged from the blogging world to challenge them, as is happening increasingly in the United States. That this should be so is taken as a compliment to their continued hegemony: probably rightly.

Further, the ability of newspapers to unmask private actions of public figures continues to have real consequences. The *News of the World*'s revelation in May 2010 that Sarah Ferguson, Duchess of York and divorced wife of Prince Andrew, the queen's second son and a trade ambassador, had sought a £500,000 bribe to influence him to assist the exports of someone she believed to be a businessman (he was a *NoW* reporter) made a large contribution to the general view of the tawdriness of the extended Windsor court.

The most potent British newspaper is that with the largest upmarket daily circulation: the *Daily Telegraph*. Its revelations in 2008 of the claiming of expenses by MPs was seen at the time as destructive of trust in elected members of parliament. This was no one-off: within a week of the new coalition government taking office in May 2010 – the paper supported the Conservatives, the dominant coalition partner – it had revealed anomalies in the claims made for expenses for a rented room in London by David Laws, a Liberal MP and former merchant banker, who had been appointed as Chief Secretary to the Treasury. This turned out to be owned by his long-term gay partner: parliamentary rules forbid such an arrangement.

Laws resigned, to widespread expressions of regret, including from leading journalists, who deemed the punishment too heavy for the crime. It emerged that the main reason for his silence about the relationship with his partner was a reluctance to allow his private sexual life to become public. Matthew Parris (2010), The *Times* commentator, commented 'what stinking hypocrisy ... to call the fall inevitable, and then wring our hands in pious lament about what a tragedy this is for the individual and the nation, as though we were helpless witnesses to some kind of extreme weather event. We in the media have been the instruments, not just the chroniclers, of the fall of a good man.'

The commercial irrelevance of scoops

The Laws affair and to a much greater degree that of the parliamentary expenses were very large news stories, which dominated the news agenda – in the latter case, for months. Yet here is an apparent anomaly: an anomaly which is presently a cancer at the heart of contemporary British journalism. In June 2010, the ABC figures reported that the *Daily Telegraph* suffered the biggest drop in circulation on year-on-year figures, from May 2009 to May 2010 – with its overall circulation dropping 16.49 per cent to a daily average of 698,456. That which has in the past been a large element in maintaining or increasing circulation – high-impact revelations – now seems to have no effect at all: one might even speculate that it had a malign effect.

That speculation gains strength from this consideration: that those newspapers whose coverage of politics, international affairs, and social issues is the fullest – *The Guardian* and *The Times* – also suffered double digit year-on-year circulation drops, of 10.47 (to 300,472) and 12.82 (to 515,379) respectively. The *Independent*, the fourth upmarket paper – though it has rebranded itself as a 'viewspaper' – had a fall of only 4.85 (to 194,501). The *Financial Times*, with the fullest international coverage but with a more specialist and a global audience, showed a fall of 2.69 (to 399,862). In the mid market, the *Daily Express* continues an even more rapid decline than the *Mirror*, by 7.79 to 663,627: the *Daily Mail*, which had shown itself more robust than most, saw its decline accelerate, by 4.83 per cent to 2,090,469,

Further still – the papers which have done best are the tabloids, *The Sun* and the *Daily Star* – the latter having been, for the previous two years, uniquely able to grow its circulation. It turned down this year, by 2.11 per cent, to 822,934 – not far below the still rapidly dropping *Daily Mirror*, down 6.58 per cent to 1,238,145. *The Sun* was the winner, with the lowest fall, of 1.61 per cent, to 2,936,099. Its Sunday stablemate, the *News of the World*, also showed a relatively small drop, 2.8 per cent to 2,858,727.

Thus the daily newspapers with the least news and the highest proportion of celebrity, show business, and scandal news are now greatly outstripping the 'heavies' – a trend underlined by the high double-digit declines of two 'heavy' Sunday newspapers, the *Observer*, by 16.10 per cent to 340,247; and the *Sunday Telegraph*, by 17.18 per cent, to 512,819. Sunday heavy market leader *Sunday Times* lost 6.42 per cent, to 1,117,749

All of these titles, with differing degrees of efficiency and success, have developed websites of great sophistication and interest, on which huge amounts of information are presented and stored and where news, analysis, and commentary is either immediately available or rapidly accessible through links. All have worked to encourage and produce debate and polemic within these sites – among which the leader remains the *Guardian*, with its early entrant, Comment is Free, a curated site in which invited writers and visitors slog it out.

Yet none make money. The *Guardian*, and its sister Sunday paper the *Observer*, have claimed the mantle of the world's leading liberal voice – a boast with substance, at least in the Anglophone world. And the newspapers' losses last fiscal year topped £60m, with few signs yet that they have been staunched.

No charge for the general

A little before this was written – in June 2010 – the News International UK titles (*The Sun, News of the World, The Times,* and *Sunday Times*) erected a pay wall around their content, and demanded a fee to read what had previously been free. There are no details available of how successful this has been: at present, there is nothing to counter the scepticism – to be sure, a self-interested scepticism – of those who have not erected pay walls, even if they may quietly hope they work.

The price charged by the News International titles is much less than the subscription to the print newspapers: and there is sense in this, for a web-based 'newspaper', shorn of the need to print and distribute, would be far cheaper than a conventional newspaper. It would be possible to retain the journalistic values and practices of a major newspaper on the web with an income of only £40m: as yet, however, we don't know if that's possible. As John Naughton (2010) wrote in the *Observer*: "There's no disagreement that people will pay – sometimes handsomely   for specialist content such as that provided by the *Wall Street Journal*, the *Financial Times* and *The Economist*, to name but three; it's the viability of general content that's in question."

Not *much* in question, among most experts. In a speech to the Westminster Forum, a media conference centre, Matt Kelly (2010), the digital content director of Trinity Mirror, argued that though newspapers boasted of as many as 30 million users a month, still they were 'mired in a deep sense of panic about the lack of accompanying revenue to pay for it all … all this content costs a fortune to create. Thirty million customers and no profit. It's not what I would call a business.' And he asked: 'can we charge successfully for general news? Not a chance. Not with the BBC pumping it out by the barrel-load free of charge. General news isn't enough. The general news business is dead. If all you have to peddle is general news, then rest in peace.'

Kelly has chosen to follow the example of the *Wall Street Journal*, the *FT* and *The Economist* and to focus on relatively small groups of customers, rather than attempting to appeal to large audiences which, though impressive in their numbers, produce no revenue. The appeal must be to 'deeply engaged' audiences, willing to pay for specialist content – as in gossip and sport. The Trinity Mirror group, which had editorial revenue streams only from its newspapers, now has twenty-eight distinct revenue streams, as it breaks out sites like 3am.co.uk (gossip) and Mirror Football.co.uk into separate businesses.

Regional papers attract less national attention, but are more affected: they have been closing at a rate of around one a week for the past two years – a trend which is forecast to accelerate. Claire Enders, who runs Enders Analysis, a media consultancy, told the House of Commons Committee on Culture, Media and Sport in June 2009 that half of the 1,300 regional titles would close in the next five years, as some £1.3bn is lost to the industry because of the collapse of the advertising market, and of circulation. At the same session of the Committee, the chief executive of D. C. Thomson, the once hugely profitable Dundee publisher – of the *Sunday Post* and the *Dundee Courier* – said it had suffered a 50 per cent drop in advertising to date. Enders also revealed the underlying difficulty for publishers depending on a web strategy: she said that a print newspaper reader was worth £100 a year – while 'the average revenue from a website visitor is £2 a year and probably falling'.

Among the regional newspaper executives who appeared with Enders, Sly Bailey of Trinity Mirror said that the company had closed twenty-seven titles in 2008 and nine in the half year to June of 2009. John Fry, chief executive of *The Scotsman* and of

Johnstone Press, said that in regional markets with three newspapers the third title was unlikely to survive, while in areas with two papers the weaker title would also close. Bailey added: 'It could be worse than that, you could have areas with no newspapers.'

As the web does not substitute for the revenue lost, nor does it appear to substitute for the news lost. Citing a US report, Enders told the Commons committee that blogs were responsible for just 4 per cent of original news content, and that 'most blogs are read by the person who created them and his close personal friends ... [they are] not a replacement for 1,300 local and regional titles' (Brook 2009). Insofar as there is a pattern to the shrinkage of the regional papers, it appears that (a) the regional Sundays remain relatively strong – that is, shrinking more slowly; (b) strong city communities, like Wolverhampton and Liverpool, have retained relatively strong daily newspapers; and (c) the London borough newspapers are declining, for the most part, more rapidly than others.

However, the largest and apparently grimmest lesson which emerges from the market conditions of both the national and the regional press is that the news which had been a staple of both national and regional papers – reports of institutions, as parliament, organisations of various kinds, local councils – now no longer commands much interest. Insofar as it does, it attracts specialist, niche demand and is increasingly covered by specialist publications and websites – some of which are able to charge a premium fee.

As Matt Kelly of Trinity Mirror explained, disaggregation of the more valuable parts of a newspaper's offering is now well advanced. Google has been the largest player here: a search engine which can aggregate news, and take the browser quickly to the content he wishes to access from different sources, destroys the special nature of any publication. Google now has a fellow in the demolition business: social networks, with Facebook in the lead. Nic Newman, former Future Media controller at the BBC, argues that social networks will 'reinforc(e) the trend towards disaggregation and put further pressure on the funding of journalism in traditional news organisations' (Newman 2009). Newman believes we are witnessing a 'historic shift in control towards individual consumers': he quotes the Wikipedia entry on social media, which describes them as 'a shift in how people read, discover and share news, information and content ... transforming monologue (one to many) into dialogue (many to many) ... transforming people from content readers into publishers'.

The future is mutual

One of the most creative responses to this emerging news ecology has been that of the *Guardian* editor, Alan Rusbridger – who, in a series of talks and articles, has sought to insert the notion of 'mutualisation' into journalistic practice. Instancing stories which the *Guardian* published with the aid of large numbers of readers – such as tax avoidance by large corporations, the death of the protestor Ian Tomlinson after an assault by a policeman during the G20 demonstrations in April 2009, the enlisting of *Guardian* readers to provide more angles and facts on MPs' expenses (the story originally broken by the *Telegraph*) – he argues that, while the conventional forms of journalism are essential to investigate, analyse and routinely cover events and institutions, 'we should (not) blind ourselves to the incredible opportunities opening up for people who don't call themselves journalists to contribute their knowledge, expertise and opinions' (Rusbridger 2009).

Rusbridger's ten principles of mutualisation are that

> *(1) it encourages participation. It invites and/or allows a response; (2) it is not an inert, us–them form of publishing; (3) it encourages others to initiate debate, publish material or make suggestions. We can follow as well as lead … (4) it helps form communities of joint interest around subjects, issues of individuals; (5) it is open to the web and is part of it … (6) it aggregates and/or curates the work of others; (7) it recognises that journalists are not the only voices of authority, expertise and interest; (8) it aspires to achieve, and reflect, diversity and well as promoting shared values; (9) it recognises that publishing can be the beginning of the journalistic process rather than the end; (10) It is transparent and open to challenge – including correction, clarification and addition.*

These are demanding injunctions on journalists used to individual working – though as Rusbridger makes clear, a number of his colleagues already use some of these practices. They also flow naturally from the developments both on the web and in journalism. They have the potential to produce a richer form of journalism, in Britain as elsewhere. If only they could be made to pay.

Newspapers, even in their shrinking state, do far more hard news reporting than broadcasters – though the latter, especially the BBC, produce a far more vivid assortment of documentaries. However, broadcast news – and especially TV news – is the dominant source for public information for most people: though here, too, there is evidence of a gradual decline, from an average of a little more than two hours a week news viewing to a little less than two hours a week in the late 2000s – with a significant upward tick in viewing figures in the past year, ascribed to concerns on the economy. The BBC's main channel, BBC1, accounts for nearly half of the news; ITV1 for about a quarter. Channel 4 news, BBC's News 24 and Sky TV account for 5–6 per cent each of news viewed (Ofcom 2007). ITV, hit by an advertising drought in 2008/9, had warned it would drop regional news: that is now unlikely. The future, however, of local and regional TV news remains unclear. Independently Funded News Consortia, media groups which would provide local and regional news and current affairs in UK regions, were announced by Ofcom in January 2009 under the then Labour government, and three groups – one each in England, Scotland and Wales – were awarded franchises. However, these new initiatives have been scrapped by Jeremy Hunt, the new Culture Secretary in the Conservative-Liberal Democrat coalition government, in favour of faster broadband access for rural areas, and an independent commercial assessment of local TV to be undertaken by Nicholas Shott, Head of UK Investment Banking at Lazard. Shott and his collaborators delivered an interim report on local TV in September, casting some doubt on the commercial viability of stand-alone commercial local TV players and encouraging a review of cross-media ownership regulation and potentials for partnerships with existing players in either television or the newspaper sector. Hunt's department will set out a local media action plan later in the year.

Change and decline in broadcasting

There has been a continued gentle decline in the number of broadcast news hours over the past decade, roughly commensurate with the decline in viewership. However, the BBC broadcasts a very high proportion – especially on BBC2 and BBC4 – of documentaries, ranging from analysis of contemporary events to recondite cultural explorations. This output, coupled with free-to-air channels available to the steadily increasing number of UK homes with digital TV or broadband services, means that high-quality explanation, analysis and learning about our world, past and present, is available in much higher quantities than at any time in the past.

The BBC, because of its size and strength, and because of its relatively secure public funding, is at the centre of almost all debates on broadcasting and broadcast news. The most high-profile attack on the BBC was that made by James Murdoch, head of News International in Europe, who argued – he is not alone in doing so – that the BBC's grip on news and its privileged funding position is throttling the life out of private-sector efforts to compete. Said Murdoch:

> *Most importantly in this all-media marketplace, the expansion of state-sponsored journalism is a threat to the plurality and independence of news provision, which are so important for our democracy. Dumping free, state-sponsored news on the market makes it incredibly difficult for journalism to flourish on the internet. Yet it is essential for the future of independent digital journalism that a fair price can be charged for news to people who value it. We seem to have decided as a society to let independence and plurality wither. To let the BBC throttle the news market and then get bigger to compensate.*

Invoking George Orwell as his inspiration, Murdoch (2009) argued that state intervention in media must become *much, much smaller;* that profits were the only guarantee of independence and accountability; and that, 'as Orwell foretold, to let the state enjoy a near-monopoly of information is to guarantee manipulation and distortion'. This line of argument is likely to strengthen – since the BBC, with a secured income, is bound to continue to appear privileged as cut-backs happen in the rest of the public sector, and impact on the private one. Further, just as News International competitors quietly hope that the pay wall will work, so they quietly hope that the BBC will be curbed – since nearly all believe that its dominance of the TV radio and news internet spheres closes off commercial competition: or, at the very least, makes it much harder.

However, a hardier perennial for the BBC, and to a degree for other broadcasters – that they are politically biased – now seems to be quiescent. There were no large rows about coverage in the last (May 2010) election – except for a stand-up, on-air row between Alastair Campbell, the former Director of Communications to Tony Blair, and Adam Boulton, the political editor of Sky News. The last five years have seen a conscious effort by the BBC to recognise where bias could appear: and a generally successful attempt to confront and end it. Television's largest coup was the staging of three debates, all of which were thought to be admirably balanced. Neutrality and objectivity in news and current affairs broadcasting, though often thought to be threatened by the popularity of biased news channels elsewhere – as Al Jazeera, Fox, and the increased power of nationally based, 24 hour global news channels such as those from China, Russia, and France – remains presently intact in the UK, while partisanship continues to flourish in national newspapers and magazines.

The availability of 24 hour news, and of instant access internet news sites, coupled with social network sites which point up news where they do not actually carry it, means that, as the increasingly current saying has it, news finds us. As Claire Enders noted, blogs do not attempt to make up for the news that are lost as local newspapers close: but the net is a huge source of information and background, which complements the news sites largely created by mainstream news organisations.

The net gains

And what of the future? Many people who have embraced the internet with enthusiasm believe it can usher in a new era of democratic openness and pluralism of opinion, as well as a vast wealth of information: at a minimum, they see it as more, or much more, useful than the mainstream media for information and accessing opinion and analysis. This is not just scholars and writers on the net, and journalists and bloggers whose professional life is largely spent on it: it applies also to more casual users. The Oxford Internet Institute, which does a bi-annual survey of the internet in Britain, showed in its last (2009) survey that trust in the net's accuracy and reliability was higher than in any of the mainstream media among net users; and even among non- or ex-users, trust was higher than in newspapers (Dutton *et al.* 2009). Net users also think that the net is much more useful for information than any other medium – by a factor of three times more than the next most useful, television (five times more useful than newspapers).

A belief in the politically and socially regenerative effects of the net has been powerfully voiced by writers such as Stephen Coleman of Leeds University's School of Communication, Charlie Beckett of the London School of Economics' Polis Institute, Bill Dutton of the Oxford Internet Institute and Yochai Benkler of the Berkman Centre for Internet and Society at Harvard University, among many others. In his *The Wealth of Networks*, Benkler (2006) celebrates the ending of control exercised by relatively few centres and individuals of media power. and their creation of a 'structure of the mass media (which) resulted in a relatively controlled public sphere – though the degree of control was vastly different depending on whether the institutional model was liberal or authoritarian – with influence over the debate in the public sphere heavily tilted towards those who controlled the means of mass communications'.

Benkler recognises that heavy-duty reporting has a rich tradition in the mainstream media: but believes that networked communication can produce journalism of an even higher quality, with the ability to go much deeper than the individual journalist, or even a team of journalists, can. One example – a relatively early one in net life – features opposition stimulated by the net to a decision by the Sinclair Broadcasting chain to air a documentary – *Stolen Honour: The Wounds that Never Heal* – a week and a half before the 2004 presidential elections: the programme was an attack on the war service of John Kerry, the Democratic presidential candidate. The mobilisation targeted not just the station's politically biased decision, but its advertisers – who began pulling their advertising, causing the company's stock to fall significantly in a rising market. Benkler underscores how, in his view, this networked activism-cum-journalism is superior to the mainstream media model, because it allows both those who have direct knowledge of a given situation and those who have a stake in change (or conservation) to exchange news and views, and to initiate or oppose action. This ability stems from the ability of everyone to see raw information, rather than that predigested by the news media.

Benkler also accepts that the net will not solve the problem of the 'rich getting richer': that is, that powerful actors will establish a much larger position on the net than weaker individuals, and that established journalists, especially those with a large mainstream media corporation behind them, will tend to dominate. But, he says, 'that is the wrong baseline'. A utopia in which 'everyone is a pamphleteer' (and everyone reads everyone else's pamphlets) is not attainable; but a much better world than that constructed by the 'one way structure of the commercial mass media' is possible; indeed, is in large parts *here*. His vision has much in common with Rusbridger's notion of mutualisation.

Wealth of networks and the poverty of choice

The vision of a world which will undergo the same series of radical social, political, and individual changes as those which the advent of printing ushered in – only faster – has been challenged, and not just by journalists resentful of a technology which seems to be ushering them down the back stairs to the tradesmen's exit. Andrew Keen's *The Cult of the Amateur* is an at times splenetic attack on the vast and undifferentiated amount of information which floods across the net, offering no editorial guides to its reliability or its source, pushing out the good stuff. Cass Sunstein's *Republic.com 2.0* highlights the propensity of net users to cocoon themselves in the tunnels of information (or prejudice) which accord with their own views, so that the experience of being exposed to views and news which challenge their worldviews – an inevitable part of watching or reading the mainstream media – is unknown. This last observation has gained in force with the revelation that many Islamist radicals, especially young men and women introduced to potentially violent forms of the ideology, spend very large amounts of time on the net, fuelling their anger and in a few cases developing the will to wreak revenge. For Sunstein (2007), a 'commons' space in which people constantly meet views and information which do not accord with their own opinions is an essential component of a liberal democracy: the filtering of unwelcome news and views from netizens' intake is, he believes, inimical to such a society. Introducing his thesis, he writes that

> the unifying issue throughout will be the various problems, for a democratic society, that might be created by the power of complete filtering. One question, which I answer in the affirmative, is whether individual choices, innocuous and perfectly reasonable in themselves, might produce a large set of social difficulties. Another question, which I also answer in the affirmative, is whether it is important to maintain the equivalent of 'street corners' or 'commons' where people are exposed to things quite involuntarily. More particularly, I seek to defend a particular conception of democracy – a deliberative conception – and to evaluate, in its terms, the outcome of a system with perfect power of filtering. I also mean to defend a conception of freedom associated with the deliberative conception of democracy and to oppose it to a conception that sees consumption choices by individuals as the very embodiment or soul of freedom.

This polarised debate between cyber optimists and cyber pessimists has tended to narrow the wide differences, so that a kind of consensus emerges – which is that 'old' and 'new' media both have their place. Commenting on the Keen/Sunstein propositions, the director of the Oxford Internet Institute, Bill Dutton (2007), writes that

> *The press, from the newspapers to broadcast media, have been at the forefront of efforts to use online journalism to reach their readers and viewers in new ways. About 30 percent of current Internet users say they read an online newspaper or news service. In this way, the Internet may be thought to be reinforcing and helping to sustain the role of the Fourth Estate. However, almost half (49%) of those who said in 2007 that they read the news online said this was different from the newspaper they read offline. About one fifth of Internet users are reading news online that they do not read offline. The Internet is therefore more realistically seen as becoming a source of news that in part complements the Fourth Estate. At the same time, citizen journalists, bloggers, researchers, politicians, government agencies and more are putting information online that provides a related, but independent, source of news as a competing alternative to the Fourth Estate.*

The future for journalism may well be contained within the optimistic views quoted above: and though they are mainly based on US models and experience, they apply more or less equally to journalism in all advanced states. But there are three reasons why those interested in the preservation – or creation, in many cases – of independent journalism should not settle for a consensus which accentuates the positive in a way which suggests that, after a bumpy period in which dyed-in-the-wool types in the mainstream media get over their fits of anxiety, everyone sees that we can all live together in peace. They should not do so, because the future for journalism – as for its past – must be constructed consciously.

Nothing works

First, and most urgent, a point made by Clay Shirky (2009) remains powerful: *nothing will work. There is no general model to replace the one the net just broke.* It may be that the net will, in the near future, attract enough advertising to give to a web-only 'newspaper' the kind of revenue it needs to maintain a large staff of reporters and editors, adequate to the task of covering a wide spectrum of news; but it seems unlikely to happen soon.

Second, it may not happen at all. That is because the nature of those newspapers which do cover a wide spectrum of news, and which have been their strength for nearly two centuries, tells against them on the web. In part this is because of the phenomenon Cass Sunstein observes: people interested in one or a few things want a lot of these things, little or nothing of the rest. The newspaper says: here are a number of pieces of information, news and opinions, culled from domestic and foreign sources, among which you can browse. Browse! The internet says: here you will find whatever information you choose. Choose! Thus the very generalness of the general newspaper fights against the path-specific logic of the net.

Third, one strength of newspapers has been their willingness to 'shadow' the public agenda. By assigning reporters to particular beats – especially politics – they have provided a quotidian commentary on centres of political power – locally, regionally, nationally, and to an extent (so far less successfully) internationally. Another strength has been their ability to analyse and report in depth – a practice which includes what's called investigative reporting. Both of these need, or at least function much better with, an organisation of some size and strength, a brand which can open doors and an institutional memory. It is of course possible that this can be done on the net, not least because it can be done much more cheaply and easily, since (to quote Shirky again) the net reduces to near zero 'the incredible difficulty, complexity and expense of making something available to the public'. But that will mean finding funding for material which is, as we've discussed, not popular enough to attract much advertising, and needs other sources of funds.

What Benkler, Dutton and others see in the net in its guise as (Dutton's phrase) 'Fifth Estate' is the ability for citizens to have a conversation, liberating them from the one-way megaphone which the mainstream media have been and to a degree remain. This conversation can at times be hugely informative, when an issue mobilises anger or curiosity or simply wide interest, and a small army of amateur researchers contribute to a rich and thick dossier of information. But at least so far, it has not developed, and may be inimical to developing, the kind of journalism which requires large resources and a substantial organisation in its support.

Yet in threatening the further existence of journalism while having little to put in its place, it may do the craft a substantial service. For the crisis it has been so influential in creating forces journalism to confront the issues of its practice, identity, and role, some of which I have described above. Those who have thought and written about this often say: we must save the news, not newspapers or news bulletins. Save journalism, not journals.

Worth the effort?

To be sure: but what journalism is worth saving? In the UK, many of the more popular newspapers have over the course of the past three decades progressively reduced the proportion of hard news they carry in favour of entertainment, scandal, and celebrity news, believing – rightly, it would seem – that this is more attractive to the bulk of their readers. Their future may be the enhancement of this, already dominant, feature into specialist publications and websites which can charge for high-grade gossip and revelations in the world of entertainment. As we have seen, the Trinity Mirror Group appears to be already well set on that road.

The criticisms which may be levelled against the practice of journalism might persuade you that it is *not* worth saving. Those below don't exhaust the field, by any means: but they seem to me to be the most important ones, which have some substance – even though in some cases they are contradictory. They include:

- an attitude towards the trade of journalism which combines both a semi-apologetic resignation to its grubbiness, and a consciousness of the sometimes malign power which journalism can wield, leading in some to an aggressive arrogance;

- an inability, or an unwillingness, to ensure that the majority of people understand what journalists themselves define as the basic information needed by citizens;

- in that journalism which claims to reflect the public agenda, a tendency to adopt the agenda of the elites, especially the political elites – and thus to be seen as part of *them* rather than sympathetic to *us*;

- in popular journalism, that consumed by most people, an increasing collapse into journalism of celebrity, scandal, and sexual revelation;

- the adoption, in the past few decades, of a professional style which emphasises journalistic independence from all social interests, leading in some cases and institutions to a style of extreme scepticism of public figures, in particular politicians;

- in part as a reaction to the above – which has been identified as a liberal or 'Western' stance – a shift from a regulated, or self-imposed, duty to objectivity, balance, and transparency towards a committed political line, and to a style which deliberately seeks to shock opponents and gather the enthusiastic support of target audiences;

- in spite of a professed commitment to independence and steely objectivity, a propensity to being captured by the agendas of governments and private interests, to the point of missing very large stories of exceptional public interest;

- an inability, in the new democracies, for the media to find a consistently independent place in society, because of their continued subordination to political, and now also to private, interests;

- even in established democracies with traditions of media independence, a limiting of the scope of media freedom by the interests of their owners, and their use as a tool to advance these owners' agendas;

- a loss of strength and confidence, as a 200-year old business model continues to decay: and while the net has hugely increased the ability of citizens to access information, it has not (yet) been able to provide a new model of journalism which covers large parts of the public agenda, and can be profitable.

It would seem that journalism is in a crisis. And so it is: even before we deal with the effects of the net. Yet in many parts of the world – as in China and Russia – journalism, conducted according to the ideals of the profession, is being practised, against the odds. It's worth asking why this is so.

The responsibility to report

Not for money: the journalism which pays well in authoritarian states is that which the powers that be like, and which tends to flatter them. Critical journalism, even when permitted, is usually done by the poorly paid. For the same reasons, it isn't done to advance one's career (as investigative journalism has done, and to a degree still does, in democratic countries): on the contrary, it can finish it. Nor does it, in general, give one power and influence, except in the limited circle of one's peers, and sometimes – as in the case of the late Anna Politkovskaya – abroad. But most such journalists in such states are unknown more widely.

It seems to be done because the people who do it develop some ethical stake in it. They see the distance between the declarations of their countries' leadership and the reality, and want to draw attention to it. They see the condition of many of their fellow citizens, and want to report on it. They realise that corruption has become general in their society, and wish to expose at least some of it in the hope that it may diminish.

They are embracing journalism as a means of holding their powers to account. They see it as a civic act. They want to develop it as a light to shine in dark places. They have, in the main, no naïve faith in its rapid efficacy: anyone who has worked as a journalist in an authoritarian state knows that, with rare exceptions, the powers that be do not respond to the revelations of independent-minded journalists, even when they do not have them pursued and harried. Yet they continue to work.

Their example points us to the necessity of independent journalism, even in welcoming and liberal climates. The UK has strongly developed traditions of journalism, and several reasons for claiming that many of its features were developed here – public service broadcasting, popular national newspapers, and literary and scientific journalism. However, it remains a relative laggard in exploring the possibilities of journalism on the net: there are few current affairs sites with more than small audiences, while much of the discussion about the future and how to shape it remains in the US. The very strengths of the mainstream media organisations, both in broadcasting and in newspaper and magazine publishing, may be an inhibition here – pointing to a web journalism future which will carry the impress of the mainstream for a long time into the future.

Kenneth Minogue, in an essay published in 2005, is right when he says that 'we cannot live without journalism' – even as he sighs over the fact. Nor, in the UK, are we likely to be asked to do so. The BBC, currently anticipating a harsher climate from a cost-cutting and often sceptical government, will remain the major producer of broadcast news and current affairs and the largest employer of journalists of different kinds. The independent broadcast sector will continue to cut news and current affairs – but no further than the bone: they will retain a skeletal domestic and international service. Sky News, still a minority viewing, seems set both to continue to expand and to retain a generally objective balance in its reporting. Newspapers will decline everywhere, but journalists will find ways – including through the use of not-for-profit and public funds – to continue doing and publishing journalism.

Minogue is also right when he describes it as 'a flow of popularised understanding' – or at any rate, he should be right, for that is what journalism should strive to achieve. It is necessary because something like journalism is needed to flow in order that most people can understand what's happening around them.

The necessary trade

The argument that a grasp of current affairs is essential to the citizen and to the proper workings of democracy has been made for a century. In the post-war period, it has been satisfied by the development of publicly owned broadcasters (which have had to tolerate varying degrees of state tutelage), by regulation of commercial broadcasters to produce public goods in the shape of current affairs programmes, and by the 'accidental' boon of newspapers, which have provided the bulk of reporting and space for comment, debate, and polemic.

Now, at a time of crisis throughout the mainstream media, the search for funding models (somewhat different from business models: the first doesn't assume a profit) is intense. A report by Len Downie, formerly editor of the *Washington Post*, and Michael Schudson, Professor of Journalism at Columbia University in New York, argued that 'what is under threat is independent *reporting* that provides information, investigation, analysis, and community knowledge, particularly in the coverage of local affairs' (Downie and Schudson 2009). They called for a range of public interventions, including changes in the designation of non-profit status so that news organisations could claim that mantle; reform of tax laws governing charitable donations and even use of federal and state funds to subsidise news – with money from telephone surcharges, Federal Communications Commission license fees, and spectrum auctions pooled into a Fund for Local News. This treats news in a similar fashion to high culture – indeed, it brackets it more or less explicitly with opera and theatre as a public good served badly by the market. Though designed for the US, these proposed solutions will take similar forms everywhere: and now need debate and experiment, for the decade just begun – the twenty-teens – will see the more rapid cull of existing mainstream media.

As Downie and Schudson recognise, news media which can fund themselves by either advertising or payments by audience are preferable to receiving state funding – since the latter may sooner or later carry explicit or implicit conditions. (Of course, all sourcing of funds carry explicit or implicit conditions, not least news produced by privately owned media corporations, but the state has larger powers than even powerful corporations.)

The UK has a better experience of public funding than most: the BBC example has seen the development of a public broadcaster whose independence, for the past four or five decades, has never been seriously attacked, nor seriously compromised. But because of independent broadcasters' retreat from news, it already finds itself in an increasingly monopolistic position. Better than relying on state funds would be continued exploration of not-for-profit support – and still better, finding new ways of selling journalism to ensure its survival as the indispensable means of describing our society and our world.

References

Benkler, Y. (2006) *The Wealth of Networks*. Yale: Yale University Press.

Brook, S. (2009). 'Half UK local and regional papers could shut by 2014, MPs are told', *Guardian*. June 16. www.guardian.co.uk/media/2009/jun/16/half-local-papers-could-shut-2014.

Downie, L., and Schudson, M. (2009) *The Reconstruction of American Journalism*. New York: Columbia Journalism School: www.columbiajournalismreport.org/.

Dutton, W. H. (2007) 'Through the Network of Networks: The Fifth Estate', University of Oxford, Inaugural Lecture.

Dutton, W. H., E. J. Helsper, and M. M. Gerber (2009) *Survey of the Internet in Britain*. Oxford: Oxford Internet Institute.

Kelly, M. (2010) Presentation at the Westminster Media Forum, London, May.

Minogue, K. (2005) 'Journalism: Power without Responsibility', *New Criterion* (Feb.): www.newcriterion.com/articles.cfm/Journalism--Power-without-responsibility -1223.

Murdoch, J. (2009) 'The Absence of Trust', MacTaggart Lecture at the Edinburgh International Television Festival 2009: www.broadcastnow.co.uk/comment/james-murdochs-mactaggart-speech/5004990.article.

Naughton, J. (2010) 'Will the Paywall Work? Thanks to Murdoch, we'll Soon Find out', *Observer* (4 July): www.guardian.co.uk/commentisfree/2010/jul/04/rupert-murdoch-paywall-times.

Newman, N. (2009) *The Rise of Social Media and its Effect on Mainstream Journalism*. Oxford: Reuters Institute for the Study of Journalism.

Ofcom (2007) *New News, Future News*. London: Ofcom.

Parris, M. (2010) 'The Foul Hypocrisy of David Laws' Downfall', *The Times* (31 May): www.timesonline.co.uk/tol/comment/columnists/matthew_parris/article714 0642.ece.

Rusbridger, A. (2009) 'I've Seen the Future and it's Mutual', *British Journalism Review*, 20 (Sept.): 19–26.

Shirky, C. (2009) 'Newspapers and Thinking the Unthinkable': www.shirky.com/weblog/2009/03/newspapers-and-thinking-the-unthinkable/.

Sunstein, C. (2007). *Republic.com 2.0*. Princeton: Princeton University Press.

8. News in Crisis in the United States: Panic – and Beyond

Michael Schudson

Introduction

Every country's media system is unique; the US media system is nonetheless an outlier among established industrial democracies. Unlike Britain and northern Europe, it has invested little in public service broadcasting and its public television has a very small audience share. Unlike most European countries, it has a relatively small national press, that is, newspapers that circulate throughout the country and whose reports and opinions colour the nation's public agenda. Until the past several decades, when a changing economy and society reduced most leading American cities from two or more newspapers to one surviving monopoly newspaper with very high profits, the American scene was dominated, city-by-city, by a competitive, thriving, metropolitan press with high readership, good profits, and occasionally high performance in terms of aggressive, brave, and probing local journalism. The local emphasis in the American press endures. Newspapers that most Americans have never seen and never heard of have larger circulations than many famous national newspapers in Europe. One of these newspapers in 2009 raised 'a huge outcry' in its community with an investigative report on a political fundraising operation run out of a state transportation agency. This was the *Orlando Sentinel* in Florida with a daily circulation of over 200,000 and more than 300,000 on Sunday (Smolkin 2009). Investigations of local corruption like this are common in these metro newspapers – at least, they have been until the economic crisis in the press of recent years. Even the so-called 'national' newspapers that have developed in the past several decades maintain a local emphasis: the *New York Times* covers metropolitan New York and New York State government while the *Washington Post* covers metro Washington with an attention that the *Guardian* and the *Telegraph* do not offer to municipal London or *Le Monde* or *Figaro* to Paris. There *is* a national press in the US but it has existed only since the 1970s. At that point the *New York Times* began to provide daily newspaper delivery in major markets around the country; the *New York Times* News Service grew as a supplier of national and foreign news to many other papers, its list of clients rising from 50 in 1960 to 500 by 1980. The *Washington Post Los Angeles Times* News Service (dissolved as a joint venture in

2009) began in 1962 and had 350 clients by 1980. In 1982 *USA Today* became the first general circulation national newspaper without a local metropolitan identity (Schudson 1995). Famously, *USA Today's* weather report covered the whole country and its sports reporting did not have a 'home team'. (In contrast to European television news, national television network newscasts in the US do not cover sports or weather but leave this entirely to local affiliates.) CNN became the first all-news cable station in 1980. National Public Radio began in 1970 and its first network news programme, *All Things Considered*, began in 1971.

The US press is somewhat unusual in other ways. Compared to France, for instance, or Italy, the upper end of the American newspaper world is not very elitist or oriented to a literate and patient readership; the lower end is not so sensational, slangy, and shameless as the popular press in Britain. The American press is more celebrated for (and self-congratulatory about) its investigative reporting than European newspapers, and also more committed in practice to objectivity than most European counterparts.

More important still in the adverse economic climate today, the US press has been more dependent on advertising revenue than European newspapers. According to data compiled by the World Association of Newspapers, American newspapers have the highest percentage of income from ad revenue among all the countries compared. Looking at specific individual newspapers for 2006, Rodney Benson found the *New York Times* received 65 per cent of its income from advertising, *Le Monde* 45 per cent (Benson 2009: 407). Dependence on advertising, combined with the recession, has flung US journalism into an economic crisis from which many European publications have been partially insulated. American newspapers have been particularly dependent on 'classified' advertising, the small announcements placed by individuals (and some businesses), announcing a used car or bicycle for sale, seeking a roommate, announcing a yard sale of old toys, clothes, and household items. Local car dealers advertise their cars, especially individual used cars, real estate agents advertise homes for sale and apartments for rent, employers large and small advertise available jobs, and private individuals advertise all manner of things in classified advertising columns. This portion of newspaper advertising has grown as a percentage of total newspaper advertising revenue – from 18 per cent in 1950 to 40 per cent in 2000 (Meyer 2008). Thus the advent of a new market for low-cost or no-cost classified advertising on internet sites like Craigslist, eBay, and monster.com (for job listings) has had a devastating impact on newspaper income. Over the past several years, the economic plight of US newspapers has raised a novel question, unthinkable earlier: when will the first major American city be without any daily newspaper?

Because the heart of American journalism has been the big-city daily newspaper serving a city and often dominating a region, not a national press blanketing the country, this is a nightmarish question. The metropolitan dailies dominate their cities, usually as monopolies; they probe corrupt city governments; they provide cohesion, community, and talking points for a city. They win Pulitzer Prizes for distinguished journalism of all sorts. The fears about the decline of these newspapers was stated memorably in one of them, the *Boston Globe* (owned by the New York Times Company but itself in financial trouble), in a story in 2008. A *Globe* reporter wrote an account of the potential death of the *Portland Press Herald* (in Maine) that quoted a 24-year-old café worker in the city: 'Can you even be a major city without a daily paper?' (deLuzuriaga 2008)

The question keeps echoing. In March 2009, the *New York Times* cited an industry analyst who said, 'In 2009 and 2010, all the two-newspaper markets will become one-newspaper markets, and you will start to see one-newspaper markets become non-newspaper markets.' Newspapers that had been in business for 150 years closed in 2009 in Denver, Colorado; in Seattle, Washington; and in Tucson, Arizona. (All of these cities at the time were two-newspaper cities.) The survival of the *Boston Globe* seemed in doubt; the Hearst Company considered closing or selling the *San Francisco Chronicle*; several major chains are today in bankruptcy proceedings. And in the closest thing to a city without a newspaper – although this has also for some time been a city of broken government, dying industry, and dwindling jobs – Detroit's jointly operated *Detroit News* and *Detroit Free Press* stopped home delivery four days a week, although citizens could purchase a print copy of the paper daily at convenience stores and newspaper boxes.

Not far from Detroit, in the home community of the University of Michigan, the *Ann Arbor News*, in business for 174 years, closed on 23 July 2009, or so it was at first announced. In fact, the paper delivers a print edition every Thursday and Sunday and provides news online daily. Is this a major city without a newspaper? This depends on what you mean by major city – the metropolitan Ann Arbor region has 300,000 people, making it the 195th largest U.S. city. It depends on what you mean by newspaper. The *Ann Arbor News* past and present has been a community newspaper, not an influential powerhouse of hard-hitting reporting. And it depends on what you mean by 'without' – is a city with a daily online newspaper that publishes a print edition twice a week 'with' or 'without' a newspaper (Perez-Pena 2009b)?

As for the *Portland Press Herald*, it still exists and employs over fifty journalists in its newsroom. The reports of the death of the American news have been exaggerated. There remain some 1,400 daily newspapers in the country.

Whether that should be cause for a sigh of relief is not clear at a time when it has become difficult even to agree on what a daily newspaper is. Does Detroit have a daily newspaper? Does Ann Arbor? Does a daily newspaper have to be printed on paper? Does it have to be printed on paper seven days a week? If it is printed on paper, does it have to be delivered to homes every day or is it still a daily newspaper if it is available at convenience stores and newsstands and is delivered to homes only a couple days a week – or not at all? Every combination and permutation of these practices is now in operation somewhere in the United States.

But that – the minimum technical requirements to call something a newspaper – is only part of the matter, and not its heart. One must consider the spirit as well as the letter of newspaper-ness: how thin can a newspaper become in terms of staffing and original content and still be functionally a newspaper? This is the question that worries publishers and editors and journalism schools and everyone else who values the role of the press in providing citizens the information and analysis they need to participate in the government of their communities and their country.

We can take this question seriously without imagining that the press of yesterday, that is, of 2005 or earlier, before the precipitous decline of newspaper income, necessarily served US democracy well. US newspapers have prospered for more than a century while consistently and dramatically under-investing in serious news coverage. In fact, the emergence of a sceptical, critical, and aggressive accountability journalism dedicated not to partisan triumph but to a sense of public service is in many respects a product of the 1960s and after. Advertising-based prosperity was a necessary condition for this journalism to emerge but it was not a sufficient condition. Prosperity had to be supplemented by two cultural changes that came with the 1960s and 1970s. The first was an increasingly widespread and fiercely defended professionalism. *Washington Post* journalist Meg Greenfield, who began her distinguished career in Washington journalism in 1961, before the transformations of the 1960s, recalled in her memoir that 'We, especially some of us in the journalism business, were much too gullible and complaisant in the old days. Just as a matter of republican principle, the hushed, reverential behavior (Quiet! Policy is being made here!) had gotten out of hand. It encouraged public servants to believe they could get away with anything – and they did' (Greenfield 2000: 88–9). Every study I know supports her observation that journalism, hardly faultless today, nonetheless became more independent of government and more committed to investigation and criticism from the Vietnam War on than ever before (Hallin 1986; Schudson 2003).

The second key outcome of the social change of the 1960s and 1970s was the presumption of publicness, the cultural impulse that democratic government should mean open government. Spurred by the televised presidential debates that began in 1960, the Freedom of Information Act of 1966, the National Environmental Policy Act's (1970) requirement that federally funded construction projects must provide environmental impact statements for public comment, and the rise in the 1970s and 1980s of a wide variety of advocacy and non-partisan non-governmental organisations that monitor different aspects of government activity, a demand for government transparency has grown apace. It is the combination of profits, professionalism, and the presumption of publicness that produced the best journalism in American history from the 1970s on.

Professionalism endures and the presumption of publicness or what is familiarly called 'transparency' grows more intense in the digital era, but profits have rapidly eroded. The result is that newspapers have slashed their budgets, closed foreign bureaux and statehouse bureaux, reduced the number of days a week they print the paper, and in the space of a half dozen years have laid off or bought out a quarter to a third of all newspaper reporters, editors, and news photographers, from new recruits to Pulitzer Prize winners. In the space of a few years the number of journalists employed in newsrooms of daily papers around the country has been reduced from just over 60,000 to somewhere in the 40,000s, probably at the low end of that (Pew Project for Excellence in Journalism 2010). The number of reporters stationed full-time in state capitals dropped from 524 in 2003 to 355 in 2009, a decline of a third (Dorroh 2009). In New Jersey, the number of full-time statehouse reporters dropped from more than fifty to just fifteen in the space of ten years (Starr 2009: 31). In New York, the Legislative Correspondents Association of journalists who covered the state government in Albany had a membership of fifty-nine reporters from thirty-one news organisations in 1981; this declined to fifty-one journalists from twenty-nine organisations in 2001, down to forty-one journalists from twenty-seven organisations in 2008 (Peters 2008). Major newspapers have cut their staffs in half – this includes the *San Francisco Chronicle*, the *Los Angeles Times*, the *Baltimore Sun*, and the *Star-Ledger* of Newark. Pile on top of that the anecdotal evidence of public officials who no longer interact with reporters not because they are avoiding them but because no reporters are dropping by to see them. Especially at the state and local levels, the press is missing.

The latest data (the 2010 Pew Project for Excellence in Journalism's report on *The State of the American News Media*) find that the decline of newsroom employment has continued apace. Their data (from the American Society of News Editors) show

2,400 full-time newsroom jobs were lost in 2007 and 5,900 in 2008. In Pew's back-of-the-envelope calculations, from 2000–10 the newspaper industry lost $1.6 billion in its reporting capacity, or 30 per cent. $141 million has been invested by private philanthropy in new media start-ups in the past four years, but this is less than 10 per cent of the losses in newspaper resources alone (Pew 2010; Fenwick 2010).

Why this rapid shrinking of the news business? A basic answer looks like this. First, young people do not read print newspapers as much as older people – or as much as younger people in times past. Even older people do not read newspapers as much as they used to, either. For people over 65, the decline has been from 72 to 65 per cent 1999–2008. For people 55–64, print readership is down from 69 to 57 per cent. It is drifting down in every age category, but most severely in the 18–24 and 24–34 groups: down from 42 to 31 per cent and 44 to 32 per cent respectively during the same 1999–2008 period (Pew 2009). Some of this is surely a drift away from news altogether. Some of it is a shift to news online. Some of it is the greater availability of news through quasi-news outlets – *The Daily Show*, Jay Leno's monologues, and so forth. Whatever the cause, the trend is unmistakable and unforgiving.

Second, newspaper companies took on a lot of debt in the past decade at exactly the wrong time. Newspapers were still a lucrative enterprise five years ago. Newspaper advertising income hit a record high of $49.4 billion in 2005 (Mutter 2008). By 2008 ad revenue was down to $38 billion, a 25 per cent decline. Newspapers had been maintaining a hefty 25 per cent operating profit, exactly what they counted on to deal with their debt, but profit was vanishing. This has to do with a third factor: the internet was stealing both readership and advertising. Why pay for a classified ad to sell your vintage LPs or your baseball cards or your grandparents' china when you can just go straight to eBay? Why sell your bike or rent your apartment in the newspaper when you can turn to Craigslist for free? And why pay the now rapidly increasing cost of a newspaper at the newsstand when you can access it from the comfort of your home or office for free, follow whatever links you wish, enhance your understanding of a story in which you have special interest with audio and visual sidebars, and quickly respond to the writer and perhaps have your response posted on the website? More and more newspaper readers now go online for their news in addition to or instead of attending to print editions, but so far online advertising has provided only a small increment for news organisations, a small fraction of their print-based advertising income (Pew 2010).

Fourth, to complete the perfect storm, the 2008–10 economic recession brought things from very bad to much worse. With US newspapers significantly more dependent on advertising revenue than most of their counterparts elsewhere around the world, their exposure to losses in a general economic downturn was swift and severe, and those with notable debt were particularly devastated.

Emerging models of news in the digital era

The intense, but confused and confusing, discussions about the future of newspapers can be grouped around three scenarios: that the old business model can be restored; that the emerging thinner journalism can survive but with much reduced profits, supplemented by for-profit and non-profit online media; and that a mixed economy for news with government, commercial, and non-profit models both competing and collaborating, can develop. Each scenario deserves some comment.

Restoration: the old business model can be restored

According to this scenario, once the economy recovers, advertising will begin to return to the newspapers, whether to the print editions or to their websites. If advertising is not sufficient, newspapers will erect 'pay walls' for their website editions. The *Financial Times*, the *Wall Street Journal*, and some local US newspapers with strong followings outside the orbit of major metropolitan regions all require payment to access some or all of their online content. The *New York Times* has announced that it, too, will establish a 'pay wall' for its popular nytimes.com in 2011, or what is referred to as a metered system – a reader may access some stories free of charge, but for additional stories, readers will be obliged to pay a subscription fee (or already be subscribers to the print edition), and there may also be a 'club' level where a subscriber gets additional benefits and uses for additional fees.

This would be the restorational model: what print or print-plus-website news organisations do is provide unique content that they distribute widely and that is paid for by advertisers to a large extent and by subscription fees to a lesser (but increasing) extent.

Could this work? Perhaps, but I think the odds are against it. The online world is very leaky. Individuals who are willing to pay for access to the *New York Times* are not likely to restrain themselves from downloading specific articles for their own use and forwarding them to friends and colleagues. One can imagine some of them (it would only take one) posting them – or posting the entire paper – to pirate sites that people could access for free. Such paying subscribers then become pirates themselves. It is hard to imagine that something like this would not happen. It could be policed by lawsuits but this would be difficult, slow, inefficient, and very unpopular.

We have long had a version of this. Individuals may be subscribers to the *New York Times* but families are the consumers. Husbands are not likely to tell their wives, or wives their husbands, to get their own subscriptions; parents are not likely to tell their children: get your own subscriptions. And room-mates may or may not tell their room-mates: get your own subscriptions. Nor have the newspapers ever complained that people share news content for free within the walls of their homes. Today it just so happens that many people live online in an expandable virtual informational home within which they share at will.

Journalism on a diet, with supplements

This is the system that has been developing over the past several years – news organisations stay in business and stay in journalism by accepting lower profits as normal and by reducing production costs to keep the books in balance. Every major regional metropolitan newspaper has cut the size of its newsroom staff, saving greatly on salaries and health insurance. A few prominent newspapers, most notably the Detroit newspapers, have sharply cut distribution costs by eliminating home delivery four of the seven days of the week. Other papers have eliminated home delivery altogether in outlying areas of their metropolitan regions.

At the same time, this very crisis, by letting go thousands of reporters and editors, has provided a workforce of talented and experienced journalists without employment and some of them have been very effective in creating online journalism organisations that have been able to quickly produce quality news reporting with small staffs, low costs, and alliances with other online organisations, with traditional newspapers and broadcasters, and with philanthropists who believe that the withering of news institutions threatens the vitality of local communities and national well-being. These new organisations are enabled not only by the relative abundance of philanthropic support in the United States and by the sudden availability of unemployed journalists of great capability but by the growing incidence of online news sources of public data that make quality reporting more possible than before for limited cost. Google is a great research assistant.

In 2010, ProPublica, one of the largest, best funded, and most expert of the new, online-only news organisations, won a coveted Pulitzer Prize for its reporting. Is this a sign of where to find journalism's future? No one knows. But, in addition to the thousands of bloggers (among the millions of blogs) who are expert in a particular area, well informed, and do original reporting, there are now several dozen philanthropically supported non-profit online news organisations across the country doing substantial public affairs journalism. There will be more. And they are working to diversify their funding – seeking advertising, tapping their own readers for voluntary contributions, and establishing partnerships with other news organisations, commercial and non-commercial alike. Whether they can find sustainable funding from their chief philanthropic sources is not yet clear. It depends on whether they prove their worth in their communities through powerful news coverage, how well the mainstream news organisations bounce back, and how the faltering economy influences the resources and priorities of the philanthropists themselves.

A mixed economy for the news

Could the US media become, to some degree, Europeanised? That is, could public funding become a more significant share of the financing for the news? This could develop in several different ways: public broadcasting could expand its news-gathering investment and the federal government could expand its financing of public broadcasting, the government could provide grants to non-profits and educational institutions that are contributing original news reporting to the media either on their own websites and other publications or in cooperation with commercial media; and the government could provide tax incentives and other changes in the legal infrastructure for media operations that would encourage new enterprise in original reporting. More ambitious proposals for government funding have been floated (Cowan and Westphal 2010; Pickard et al. 2009; Downie and Schudson 2009; McChesney and Nichols 2010) but there is little support for them.

Most American journalists resist the idea of government financial support for the news media. They think that any government assistance to the press automatically violates the First Amendment. (It does not – if it did, there would be no Public Broadcasting Service or National Public Radio.) They believe government aid is unprecedented. (It is not. The federal government underwrote the growth of the news industry from early on. The strong faith of the American founders in the role of the circulation of information in sustaining a republic led to the Postal Act of 1792 that established a system of post offices and roads connecting them, and singled out newspapers for special low-cost mailing privileges.) Many American journalists are not only ill informed about their own history but are insistently and insouciantly unwilling to examine systems of press subsidy in European democracies. Neither the BBC, well known in the US, nor other public service broadcasting systems are much discussed in the US debates on the future of news, and the direct government subsidies to newspapers or to journalists themselves in Sweden, Norway, Denmark, Finland, France, and elsewhere are almost never mentioned. Academic studies of these systems, though they differ in their judgements of how effective the subsidies have been in maintaining the number and variety of news outlets, nowhere suggest that subsidies have reduced the independent spirit of the subsidised papers (Weibull 2003; Picard and Grönlund 2003; Murschetz 1998).

Which of these three general models holds keys to the future for American journalism? In my own judgement, I think the road to 'restoration' is blocked. Even if pay walls can be made to work, by no means a settled question, they are the online equivalent of paid subscriptions, and paid subscriptions in the United States account for just a quarter or a third of newspaper receipts. There would still be a need to bring in a large amount of online advertising. Perhaps this will happen, but so far it is not emerging.

Meanwhile, the road to the 'mixed economy' is lined with political roadblocks. There is little political support for 'bailing out' the newspaper business. Modest government initiatives may have a chance and could make a difference. The government could invest more in journalism education as it does in other professional education and in higher education generally; government can invest more in the construction of databases that can be publicly available to journalists and others and this could help reduce the costs of news gathering and improve the quality of news. The government can streamline the tax codes to make it easier to launch non-profit news organisations or to transform conventional commercial news organisations into non-profits or 'low-profit' corporations with corresponding tax advantages. The government could also invest more heavily in the Corporation for Public Broadcasting, in a way that would enable National Public Radio, the most successful radio news operation in the country, to sharply increase its local news coverage. All of these measures would help. But even taken together it is inconceivable to me that they would come close to the level of government aid that many European democracies provide. Short of a fundamental rethinking that has barely begun, the road to a 'mixed economy' model is a very long one.

Until such a change of mind and heart makes government support more palatable in the United States, we are likely to see more of what we see already: mainstream journalism on a diet, with dietary supplements provided by a small but growing entrepreneurial, experimental, and in most cases non-profit, online media sector. This is not a hopeless scenario, so long as independent online media can gain some traction. But can they? Yes, but their success depends on individual passion – the presence of which is both unmistakable and inspiring in the new online sector – on the willingness of hundreds and thousands of journalists and would-be journalists to pursue their craft with little prospect of earning a good living at it, and on the willingness of more philanthropists to reconsider their priorities and add, to their already long list of worthy causes, the watchdog press.

Implications for democracy

Journalists frequently proclaim that a free press contributes to and is essential to the functioning of democracy. In general, Americans outside journalism do not have fundamental doubts about this, however much they complain about the media. Demonstrating the efficacy of news in democracy, however, is not so easy.

Nor is it easy to be very specific about what – precisely – contributing to democracy means. What is it about journalism that democracy needs? Does democracy need the weather report? Sports coverage? News of fashion, of births and deaths and marriages? Recipes and announcements about the opening of new restaurants? If these features do not directly contribute to self-government, do they do so indirectly by subsidising less popular but more democratically essential news stories? Do people buy a general news product for the sports or the sex scandal but then stay, on occasion, for political or social news that makes them more informed citizens?

As for political news: how much and what sort does a democracy require? Do we need as much coverage of legislatures as the press provided a decade ago before newsroom downsizing became common or before the past few years when newsroom shrinkage began cascading? How much and what sort of coverage of law-making and executive performance does democracy require?

There are no less than six distinguishable ways that the media have in different times and places functioned to aid democracy (for a fuller discussion, see Schudson 2008: 11–26). Some, but not all, have been weakened in the current economic crunch.

First, journalism has an educational function, informing the public – the ultimate democratic authority – of what its political representatives are doing, what dangers and opportunities for society loom on the horizon, and what fellow citizens are up to, for better and for worse. News tells us things we would not otherwise know about matters of general public concern. This has not always been taken for granted. In the eighteenth century, even representative legislatures and assemblies operated largely in secret from the people who elected them. Freedom of the press meant – and this was not a small thing – freedom for a writer to speak his opinion as he wished, even in criticism of the government. But it did not mean a freedom to report. Indeed, reporting – that is, the effort of the printers who operated newspapers to affirmatively and routinely seek out news and to hire people to do so (as opposed to reprinting items from other papers and printing whatever readers voluntarily contributed) dates in the United States to the early nineteenth century, not to the early eighteenth century when the first newspapers (weekly publications concerning contemporary affairs) in the American colonies began. The features of the US press most energetically defended in journalism circles as essential to democracy are features that were largely unknown to those who secured passage of the First Amendment in 1791.

Second, journalism has an investigative or 'watchdog' function. News becomes a theatre in which conflicts inside government are played out on a public stage – regardless of whether the public audience is large or small. Journalism can perform its institutional role as a watchdog even if nobody in the provinces is following the news. All that matters is that people in government believe they are following the news. If an inner circle of attentive citizens is watchful, this is sufficient to produce in the leaders a fear of public embarrassment, public controversy, legal prosecution, or fear of losing an election. The job of the media, in this respect, is to make powerful people tremble. The watchdog function of the press has a negative orientation; it is designed to foil tyranny rather than to forward new movement or new policy, it holds government officials to the legal and moral standards of public service. If the virtue of the informative journalist is judgement, the virtue of the investigative journalist is suspicion.

Third, journalism offers analysis. This is an effort to explain a complicated scene in a comprehensible narrative. Few US news organisations invest in it to any large degree.

Those that have done so – leading metropolitan daily newspapers, a dozen magazines, and the more ambitious efforts of national television networks and National Public Radio – have all been hit hard by the industry's economic downturn. The primary engines of public investigation and analysis are at risk.

Fourth, journalism can encourage social empathy. This deserves more attention in the rhetoric about journalism as a civic enterprise. Journalism informs the most engaged and empowered citizens, people who vote and those who have the leverage to turn society in one direction or another, about neighbours and fellow citizens they may not have direct access to. Our best news organisations do more of this and do it better than ever. Coverage of Hurricane Katrina was rich, passionate, and compassionate in many news outlets. With the *New York Times*, it was also persistent. The *Times* assigned a 'Katrina editor' and followed up the disaster with story after story, nearly every week, for the next year, with continuing coverage long after that, following the story not only in New Orleans and along the Gulf Coast but in Houston and Atlanta and other communities where hurricane victims relocated. Human interest stories have been a part of journalism for a long time but they are used more and more instrumentally these days, to draw readers or viewers into a larger tale, one that tells us not just about an interesting or unusual individual but shows us how that person's experience links up with larger issues.

Fifth, journalism offers a public forum. From the early days of journalism to the present, newspapers have made space for letters to the editor. In the US for forty years, leading newspapers also have provided an 'op-ed' page – so named because it is the page opposite the editorial page – in which staff writers, syndicated columnists, and guest columnists, experts as well as ordinary citizens, provide a variety of views on current issues. But it seems beyond question that the public forum function of journalism has cracked wide open with the creation of the World Wide Web; the internet opens up this journalistic function in the most wide-ranging and profound way. Its virtue is not individual but social, the virtue of interaction, of conversation, of an easy if sometimes coarse and contentious democratic sociability.

Finally, journalism serves democracy as an advocate for various viewpoints, issues, and policies, and no form of journalism has been more important historically than partisan journalism. Even in US journalism, widely recognised elsewhere in the world for its powerful commitment to notions of non-partisanship and objectivity, party-based journalism dominated the past, seeking to rally those who share the journalist's political or ideological position. This was the main form of journalism in the US throughout the nineteenth century. There is much to be said for journalism as partisan cheerleader, journalism as exhortation and incitement to participate. If different partisan viewpoints are well represented among institutions of journalism, then a journalist-as-advocate model may serve the public interest very well. Partisan journalism enlists the heart as well as the mind of the audience. It gives readers and viewers not only information but a cause, not only something to read but a reason to care.

What has been the impact of the current economic transformation of the news business on the capacity of news to serve these six functions?

1. The internet that has savaged the traditional economic model of the press has both weakened and strengthened the informational, watchdog, analytical, and social empathy functions. By undermining the economic survivability of the leading organisations that undertake the most and the best informational,

investigative, analytical, and serious social empathy news, the internet has weakened the democratic value of the press. By providing vast amounts of government information and other useful databases online, by making 'search' a more adaptable function for the ordinary citizen, by enabling individuals with access to the internet to scan a wide variety of news outlets and not just the monopoly newspaper of the city they live in, and by stimulating the imaginations and ambitions of countless individuals who see opportunity in the newly available low-cost access to worldwide audiences, the internet has at the same time enlarged the communicative competences of democracy. The losses are great – but the gains are also beginning to add up.

2. The internet greatly expands the public forum function. One might even say that what had become something of a vestigial function up until the expansion of opinion journalism on talk radio and cable television in the 1980s and 1990s, has been powerfully revitalised in online media.

3. The internet offers new opportunities for mobilising for democratic participation. So does the move of some cable television channels (FOX News and MSNBC) to a journalism more like the partisan press of the nineteenth century than the professionalised press of the past half century. This may ultimately prove a democratic benefit, but it is not necessarily benign. It would be tragic if the professionalised press were to be decimated, leaving nothing but partisan ranters whose enthusiasms or hatreds overpower their scruples and sense of fairness. Many people fear this is where the US media are rapidly tending, but I do not judge the situation anywhere near so dire.

In sum, the losses to democracy are real, if impossible to calculate. And they may be greatest, as Paul Starr (2009) has suggested, in local and state news reporting, not in national and foreign reporting. The news functions that require the greatest investment in the time and skill of journalists and the resources of their news organisations – investigation, analysis, and social empathy – are the parts of journalism most in jeopardy. They often require persistence and even courage, not only on the part of the reporter but on the part of the news organisation that hires the investigative journalists and that may be asked to stand behind them, even in the courtroom if necessary.

References

Benson, R. (2009) 'What Makes News More Multiperspectival?', *Poetics*, 37: 402-418.

Cowan, G., and Westphal, D. (2010) 'Public Policy and Funding the News', Los Angeles: University of Southern California Center on Communication Leadership and Policy: available at www.fundingthenews.org.

DeLuzuriaga, Tania (2008) 'A Maine Beacon Blinks', *Boston Globe* (15 Aug.).

Dorroh, J. (2009) 'Statehouse Exodus', *American Journalism Review* (April/May).

Downie, L., and Schudson, M. (2009) *The Reconstruction of American Journalism*. New York: Columbia Journalism School: http:/www.columbiajournalismreport.org.

Fenwick, A. (2010). 'State of the Media, by the Numbers', *Columbia Journalism Review* (15 March): www.cjr.org/the_news_frontier/state_ of_the_media_by_the_numb. php?page=all&print=true

Greenfield, M. (2000) *Washington* (New York: Public Affairs Press).

Hallin D. C. (1986) *'The Uncensored War': The Media and Vietnam*. New York: Oxford University Press.

McChesney, R. W., and Nichols, J. (2010) *The Death and Life of American Journalism*. New York: Nation Books.

Meyer, P. (2008) 'The Elite Newspaper of the Future', *American Journalism Review*. (Oct./Nov.).

Murschetz, P. (1998) 'State Support for the Daily Press in Europe: A Critical Appraisal', *European Journal of Communication*, 13: 291–313.

Mutter, A. (2008). 'Reflections of a Newsosaur': http://newsosaur.blogspot.com (21 Dec.).

Perez-Pena, R. (2009a) 'As Cities Go from Two Papers to One, Talk of Zero', *New York Times* (12 March): A1.

— (2009b) '4 Michigan Markets Will Lose Daily Newspapers, as Ailing Industry Tries to Cope', *New York Times* (23 March).

Peters, J. (2008) 'As Newspapers Cut Costs, a Thinning of the Guard among Albany's Press Corps', *New York Times* (8 Oct.): A29.

Pew Project for Excellence in Journalism (2009) *State of the News Media 2008*: www.journalism.org.

— (2010) *State of the News Media 2009*: www.journalism.org.

Picard, R. G., and Grönlund, M. (2003) 'Development and Effects of Finnish Press Subsidies', *Journalism Studies*, 4: 105–20.

Pickard, V., Stearns, J., and Aaron, C. (2009) *Saving the News: Toward a National Journalism Strategy*. Washington, DC: FreePress.net: www.freepress.net.

Schudson, M. (1995) *The Power of News*. Cambridge, Mass.: Harvard University Press.

— (2003) *The Sociology of News*. New York: W. W. Norton.

— (2008) *Why Democracies Need an Unlovable Press*. Cambridge, UK: Polity Press.

Smolkin, R. (2009) 'Cities without Newspapers', *American Journalism Review* (June/July): 18–25.

Sokolove, M. (2009) 'What's a Big City without a Newspaper?', *New York Times Magazine* (9 Aug.).

Starr, P. (2009) 'Goodbye to the Age of Newspapers (Hello to a New Era of Corruption)', *New Republic* (4 March): 28–35.

Weibull, L. (2003) 'The Press Subsidy System in Sweden', in N. Couldry and J. Curran (eds.), *Contesting Media Power*. Lanham, Md.: Rowman & Littlefield, 89–107.

9. The Changing Landscape of Brazil's News Media

Mauro P. Porto

Introduction

The aim of this chapter is to analyse the main trends in Brazil's media landscape, with a focus on the status of news organisations.[1] This analysis can shed new light on contemporary debates about the future of the news media and its impact on democracy. Discussions about journalism's prospects are often based on developments in the United States and Western Europe, failing to fully consider other contexts, especially those emerging in the global South. The evolution of Brazil's news media demonstrates, however, that trends taking place in post-industrial countries cannot be generalised to other parts of the world.

Several specificities of the Brazilian context point to the limits of generalisations based on Western understandings of current developments in news organisations. Brazil's media system remains dominated by broadcast television, while the penetration of new technologies, such as the internet and pay TV (cable and satellite), has remained relatively restricted. As a result, narratives about the rise of a 'post-network era' have limited applicability. Moreover, the circulation of Brazilian newspapers has increased significantly in recent years, indicating that arguments about the 'death of newspapers' are premature. On the other hand, some of the most intense competition in the media sector is not simply between commercial media conglomerates, but also between these players and media outlets controlled by religious groups, such as TV Record. This chapter argues that Brazil's media system, despite being subject to some of the same technological and economic forces that challenge news organisations elsewhere, is developing in a very different direction from what American and European discussions might lead one to expect. As discussed below, recent trends in Brazil's socio-economic context, especially in terms of the declining levels of poverty, social inequality, and illiteracy, help explain key patterns in the evolution of the news media.

[1] I am thankful to David Levy and Rasmus Kleis Nielsen for their comments and suggestions to an earlier version of this chapter. I am, however, the only one responsible for its shortcomings. I would also like to thank the Brazilian Association of Subscription Television (Associação Brasileira de Televisão por Assinatura, ABTA) for the assistance in obtaining data about the pay TV market in Brazil.

After describing the main features of Brazil's broadcasting and print media sectors, the chapter identifies key pressures facing news organisations. I argue that the financial difficulties that Brazilian news organisations currently face have roots in the late 1990s and early 2000s, when the economic context changed dramatically after the devaluation of the national currency. On the other hand, recent and positive shifts in Brazil's social indicators (poverty, social inequality, and illiteracy) open new opportunities for the media sector. The chapter concludes with a discussion of the main responses to these pressures by policy-makers and media companies, stressing their implications for the role of journalism in Brazilian democracy.

The broadcasting sector

One of the most important features of the Brazilian case is the centrality of broadcast television in the media system. Contrary to patterns found in wealthier nations, the penetration of new technologies, such as pay TV (cable and satellite) and the internet, has been significantly limited in Brazil. Figure 9.1 presents the penetration of different media and technologies in Brazilian households over a thirteen-year period. It shows the strong and steady diffusion of television, from 86 per cent of the households in 1997 to 94 per cent in 2009. In the same period, the evolution of pay TV technologies was not only more limited in scope, but also sluggish. As Figure 9.1 shows, pay TV penetration has remained stagnant around 12 per cent of the households, contradicting initial predictions that these new technologies would radically change the communication landscape in Brazil, bringing an end to the dominance of broadcast television (Duarte 1996; Hoineff 1996). As the revolutionary impact of new technologies was being celebrated in the 1990s, a few dissenting voices highlighted that social inequality and income concentration would remain powerful obstacles to the expansion of new technologies in Brazil (Porto 1999; Straubhaar 1996).

Figure 9.1. Penetration of different media and technologies in Brazilian households (% of all households)

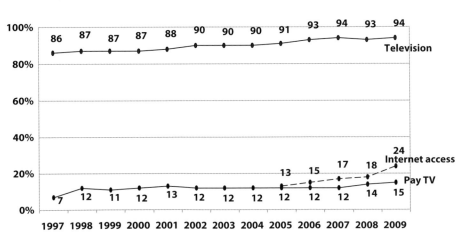

Data about penetration of television sets comes from Grupo de Mídia São Paulo, Mídia Dados (1999–2009 editions).
Data about the penetration of pay TV comes from Associação Brasileira de Televisão por Assinatura (ABTA). Data about internet penetration comes from Centro de Estudos sobre as Tecnologias da Informação e da Comunicação (CETIC), http://www.cetic.br.

Figure 9.2. Reach and individual ratings of broadcast television in Brazil between 6.00 p.m. and midnight (%)

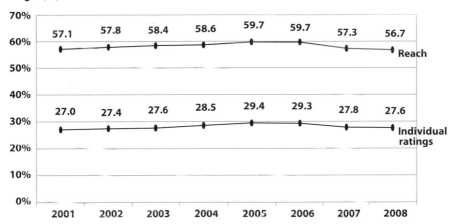

Data from IBOPE, Painel Nacional de Televisão (National Television Panel), as presented by Parente (2009), Reach (Alcance) refers to the percentage of individuals that watched at least one minute of television in a specific time slot. Individual ratings (Audiência Individual – AI) refer to the average of individuals that watched television during a specific time slot. IBOPE's National Television Panel collects audience data in Brazil's ten largest markets.

Contrary to patterns found in post-industrial nations, especially the United States, national broadcast television in Brazil has not experienced a linear and continuous decline of its share of the national audience. Figure 9.2 presents the evolution of the 'reach' and 'individual ratings' of television in Brazil between 6.00 p.m. and midnight.[2] It shows that television viewership remained remarkably stable over the eight-year period. In the case of Brazil, the rise of new technologies has not undermined the dominant position of free to-air television. According to Dora Câmara, Director of IBOPE Institute's Commercial Department, audience ratings data suggests that '[p]eople are sharing their time with the internet, without abandoning television' (cited by Parente 2009, my translation). The same popularity of broadcast television can be found among pay-TV subscribers. Audience data show that television networks attract a bigger audience than cable and satellite channels, even among those who can afford a pay-TV subscription.[3]

Besides penetration and ratings, the centrality of broadcast television in Brazilian society can also be seen in the distribution of advertising revenues. Brazil is one of the ten largest advertising markets of the world, but expenditure is highly concentrated in broadcast television (Sinclair 2009). Table 9.1 presents the share of advertising according to type of media. It shows that the advertising market is highly concentrated on free-to-air television. In the last decade, the TV networks have absorbed on average more than 59 per cent of all advertising revenues in Brazil. Other traditional media – such as newspapers, magazines, and radio – had their share reduced, generating significant constraints for their future growth. Besides terrestrial television, the only media to have increased their share of advertising in the period were pay TV and the internet.

[2] Reach (*Alcance*) refers to the percentage of individuals that watched at least one minute of television in a specific time slot. Individual ratings (*Audiência Individual,* AI) refer to the average of individuals that watched television during a specific time slot.
[3] Data collected in 2008 from households with pay TV (cable or satellite) shows the dominance of network programming, especially during prime time. For example, from 9.00 p.m. to 10.00 p.m., when most TV sets are on, an average 22% of households watched one of the television networks, while only 7% watched cable or satellite channels (Grupo de Mídia São Paulo, *Mídia Dados 2009*, p. 276).

Table 9.1. Distribution of advertising investments in Brazil, according to type of media (%)

	2001	2002	2003	2004	2005	2006	2007	2008	2009
Television	57.8	60.3	59.0	59.2	59.6	59.4	59.2	58.8	60.9
Newspapers	21.7	20.5	18.1	16.6	16.3	14.7	16.4	15.9	14.1
Magazines	10.8	10.0	9.4	8.3	8.8	8.6	8.5	8.5	7.7
Radio	4.9	4.7	4.5	4.3	4.2	4.2	4.0	4.2	4.4
Pay TV	1.6	2.0	1.7	2.2	2.3	3.5	3.4	3.7	4.4
Internet	–	–	1.5	1.6	1.7	2.1	2.8	2.7	4.3
Others	4.3	4.8	5.7	5.6	7.5	6.0	8.8	5.3	8.3

Data from Associação Nacional dos Jornais, http://www.anj.org.br. Please note that the ANJ figures used here differ from the WARC figures used in Figure 1.4.

There is therefore overwhelming evidence that broadcast television remains the dominant medium, contrary to trends in parts of the post-industrial world. Since the 1980s, wealthier nations have experienced a rapid dissemination of new technologies, such as cable television and the internet. Several scholars have deployed the term 'post-network era' to describe the rise of this more fragmented and decentralised media environment (e.g. Lotz 2007). However, studies of the 'post-broadcast era' that adopt a broader comparative approach suggest that changes in the television industry have been highly uneven and that we should avoid unreflective applications of categories from Anglo-American studies to understand processes taking place in other regions (e.g. Turner and Tay 2009). In fact, a recent study of trends in world television concluded that national broadcast television is still the dominant framework for news and for cultural forms in most countries (Straubhaar 2007).

Radio is an important medium in Brazil, with 1,707 AM stations and 2,281 FM stations nation-wide and a 91.5 per cent penetration of households.[4] Several radio networks have strong journalism departments, including Rede Bandeirantes and CBN. However, Brazil's radio industry has not developed a national character and its fragmented audiences tend to use it mostly for musical entertainment, instead of as a news source (Straubhaar 1996). Due to these reasons and limitations of space, the analysis that follows does not consider the role of radio.

The dominance of TV Globo

While broadcast television is the central medium in Brazil, TV Globo (Rede Globo) is the dominant force in the communications sector. TV Globo is the largest communications company in Brazil and in 2005 it was ranked as the twenty-sixth largest media conglomerate in the world, with an annual revenue of $2.6 billion (Straubhaar 2007: 99). The network is part of Globo Organisations, a family-owned conglomerate that started when journalist Irineu Marinho launched the newspaper *O Globo* in 1925. In the following decades, Irineu Marinho's son, Roberto Marinho

---

[4] Grupo de Mídia São Paulo, *Mídia Dados Brasil 2009*, pp. 304–7.

(1904–2003), built a media empire with interests in all sectors of the cultural industries, including newspapers (*O Globo*, *Extra*), news-magazines (Época), radio (Rádio Globo, CBN), cable television (NET), film (Globo Filmes), music (Som Livre), publishing (Editora Globo), and the internet (Amaral and Guimarães 1994; Brittos 2000; Sinclair 1999; Wilkin 2008). TV Globo's first channel was launched in 1965 and the company established its dominant position during the military dictatorship (1964–85), when the Marinho family developed a close alliance of interests with the authoritarian regime, supporting its project of national and economic integration (Lima 1988; Sinclair 1999; Straubhaar 1989). After the transition to democracy in 1985, conservative media mogul Roberto Marinho often used his media empire to intervene in the political process and TV Globo became known for its partisan character (see Porto 2003). However, in the mid-1990s, when Brazil's process of democratisation advanced and Marinho's three sons took over the administration of the conglomerate, TV Globo went through a process of opening, becoming less partisan and more representative of societal viewpoints (Porto 2007b).

TV Globo remains the dominant force in Brazil's communication landscape, but its market position has been facing stronger challenges in more recent periods. Figure 9.3 presents the share of the national television audience by network. The data show that in the thirteen-year period TV Globo has maintained a strong lead, with an average of 53 per cent of the national audience. However, TV Globo's ratings have been declining since 2005 and reached a record low of 44 per cent of the national audience in 2008.

As Figure 9.3 shows, one of the most important shifts in Brazil's television industry, which helps explain the relative decline of TV Globo, is the recent rise of TV Record (Rede Record) as the second largest network. TV Record started in 1953 and became popular in the 1960s through its legendary musical festivals, but it started to face a decline with the emergence of TV Globo as the leading network in the late 1960s and early 1970s. In 1990, TV Record was purchased by the Universal Church of the Kingdom of God (UCKG), a neo-Pentecostal church led by Bishop Edir

Figure 9.3. Share of the national audience (7.00 a.m.–midnight), according to television network (%)

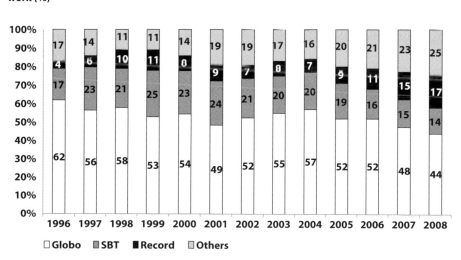

Data from Grupo de Mídia São Paulo, Mídia Dados (1999–2009).

Macedo (Birman and Lehmann 1999; Reis 2006). Founded in 1977, UCKG has been characterised by the intense use of the media and by a rapid growth in a country that had been historically dominated by Catholicism. By the 1990s, the UCKG had more than two million followers in Brazil and became a global phenomenon, with branches in more than eighty countries (Mariano 2004). The purchase of TV Record by UCKG reveals a peculiarity of the communications sector in Brazil: the significant growth of media outlets owned by religious groups, including the Catholic Church (Lima 2001: 100–11; Santos and Capparelli 2004). In the midst of a battle for followers and viewers, TV Record and TV Globo became strong opponents, sometimes engaging in open and over-the-air confrontations (Birman and Lehmann 1999; Reis 2006). The competition between TV Globo and TV Record is not only commercial in nature. It also reflects the growing hegemonic crisis of Catholicism in Brazil and of an elite-centred definition of national identity that tends to marginalise Brazilians with lower levels of income and education.[5]

Although UCKG owns TV Record, the network is run for the most part as a relatively independent commercial operation. Religious programmes are usually restricted to late night and early morning hours. TV Record has challenged TV Globo through news, reality shows, and the production of *telenovelas*, successfully becoming the second largest network in 2008. As Figure 9.3 shows, until then the second place had been historically monopolised by SBT (Sistema Brasileiro de Televisão), the television network launched in 1981 by entertainer Silvio Santos. In the 1960s and 1970s, Santos became a popular host of variety shows, which were aired by several networks, including TV Globo. He managed to build the second largest network by targeting the lower classes with 'popular' programmes, including game shows and tabloid news, as well as by importing Mexican *telenovelas* (Mira 1995).

Brazil's broadcasting sector is controlled by an oligopoly of private companies, while state-controlled media, often called 'public' or 'educational', remain marginalised, with low levels of viewership. Brazil's 'educational' media sector, which includes radio and television stations owned by the states and by the federal government, was launched by a decree of the military dictatorship in 1967 (Bolaño and Brittos 2008). Most media outlets that make up the so-called 'public' system are in fact state-owned, lacking the financial and administrative autonomy that characterises public broadcasting systems elsewhere. The main exception is TV Cultura in the state of São Paulo, which is administered by a public foundation. In December 2007, President Luiz Inácio Lula da Silva centralised all stations of the 'educational' system by creating the Brazil Communication Corporation (Empresa Brasil de Comunicação – EBC). The new corporation was put in charge of TV Brasil, a new national television network that links state-owned stations. Although Lula's administration has presented the creation of EBC and TV Brasil as a strengthening of the public media sector, the system that emerged lacks autonomy from the federal government, since the members of its board of directors, including those supposed to represent civil society organisations, are appointed by the president (Bolaño and Brittos 2008).

Brazil's broadcasting sector is characterised by concentration of ownership, the predominance of family groups, a marginal state-owned system, and the significant influence of religious interests. The dominant position of television as a medium and

---

[5] The growth of the UCKG has taken place predominantly among the urban poor and the Church's questionable fundraising practices have been the object of media exposés and legal investigations. However, much of the criticism of the UCKG reflects a class bias that presents its followers as ignorant or easily manipulated (see Birman and Lehmann 1999).

of TV Globo as a media group means that its primetime newscast *Jornal Nacional* remains Brazilians' most important news source (Porto 2007a).

The print media sector

One of the reasons for the dominance of broadcast television in Brazil has been the historical low levels of circulation of print media. Similarly to Southern Europe (Greece, Italy, Portugal and Spain), Latin America has been characterised by low levels of newspaper circulation and journalistic professionalisation, as well as by a tradition of instrumentalisation of private media by their owners (Hallin and Papathanassopoulos 2002). But even though the historical tradition of a politically active press can be felt to this day (see Albuquerque 2005), the Brazilian print media sector has experienced a significant process of modernisation, with higher levels of professionalisation and more balanced patterns of political coverage (Azevedo 2006; Matos 2008; Porto 2003).

Brazil has a vibrant print media sector, with more than 500 dailies and three major weekly news-magazines. Table 9.2 presents the daily newspapers and the weekly news-magazines with the highest circulation in Brazil. The data show once again the dominant position of Globo Organisations. Two of the best-selling newspapers (*O Globo* and *Extra*) and one of the main news-magazines (Época) are owned by the Marinho family. The daily with the highest circulation, *Folha de S. Paulo*, has been owned by the Frias family since 1962. Founded in 1875, *O Estado de S. Paulo* is one of the oldest and more traditional newspapers in Brazil and since 1902 it has been owned by the Mesquita family. The most important elite-oriented, quality papers are considered 'national' publications, but they have in fact a regional character, since their circulation is concentrated in the south-east and south, the most developed and urbanised regions.

The list of the best-selling publications also shows the growing importance of tabloids in Brazil. Besides Globo Organisations' *Extra*, the popular dailies *Super Notícia* and *Meia Hora* have joined the selective group of publications with the highest circulation. Both papers have appeared recently and illustrate the meteoric rise of tabloids in Brazil. *Super Notícia* was launched in 2002 by Sempre Editora, the group that publishes the quality newspaper *O Tempo* in the state of Minas Gerais. The newspaper *Meia Hora* was launched in 2005 by Grupo O Dia Comunicação, the

Table 9.2. Newspapers and news magazines with the highest circulation in Brazil

Newspapers	Type	Average daily circulation (2009)	News magazines	Average weekly circulation (2008)
Folha de S. Paulo	Quality paper	295,558	Veja	1,089,900
Super Notícia	Tabloid	289,436	Época	420,500
O Globo	Quality paper	257,262	Isto É	405,100
Extra	Tabloid	248,119		
O Estado de S. Paulo	Quality paper	212,844		
Meia Hora	Tabloid	185,783		

Newspaper circulation data comes from Araripe (2010).
News-magazine circulation data comes from Grupo de Mídia São Paulo, Mídia Dados.

company that also publishes the tabloid *O Dia*, one of the oldest and most important popular papers in Brazil. *O Dia* first appeared in 1951 and in 1983 it was purchased by journalist Ary Carvalho. In April 2010, the family Carvalho sold the company Grupo O Dia Comunicação to the Portuguese conglomerate Ongoing Media Group.

Table 9.2 also points to the prominent position of weekly news-magazines in Brazil's media system. The newsmagazine *Veja* has a significant circulation, with more than one million copies sold per week. The magazine is owned by Grupo Abril, one of the largest publishing and electronic media groups in Latin America, which also owns TVA, a cable television company, and MTV Brazil. Besides Globo Organisations' *Época*, which was launched in 1998, *Isto É* is another important news source. It has been published since 1976 by the media group Editora Três.

Growth of circulation via tabloidisation

Newspapers in the United States and other developed nations have experienced a steady decline in circulation, often attributed to the loss of readers to the internet and other new media. The Brazilian case demonstrates, however, that trends taking place in the US and Western Europe cannot be generalised to other parts of the world. In fact, newspaper circulation has increased in Brazil recently. Figure 9.4 presents trends in the circulation in Brazilian newspapers between 2000 and 2008. The data show a steady growth of circulation after 2004, with the record high of 72.5 copies sold daily per 1,000 adults in 2008.[6] It should be noted, however, that sales declined in 2009. Newspaper circulation dropped 3.5 per cent from 2008 to 2009, due mostly to the global financial crisis, which contributed to slow economic growth in Brazil (Araripe 2010; Molina 2010; Silva 2010).

Figure 9.4. Average newspaper circulation in Brazil (copies sold daily per 1,000 adult inhabitants)

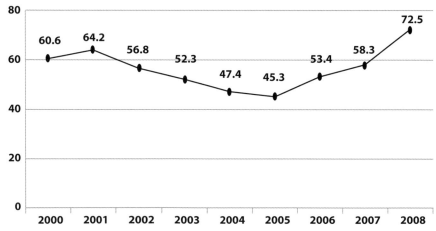

Data from World Association of Newspapers, World Press Trends.

[6] As noted above, newspaper circulation in Latin America in general and in Brazil in particular is quite low by international standards. However, Brazil's average (72.5) is almost half of that of post-industrial nations like France (152.1), which have more favorable socio-economic conditions for the expansion of newspaper readership (circulation data come from WAN 2009).

Figure 9.5. Share of circulation of top 10 newspapers in Brazil, according to type (quality papers vs. tabloids)

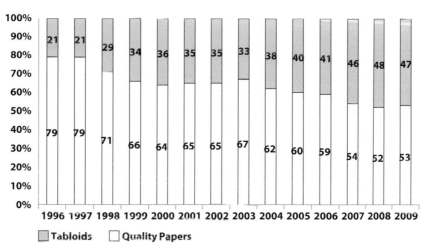

The numbers from 1996 to 2008 were calculated by the author based on data presented by the reports from Grupo de Mídia São Paulo (Mídia Dados, 1999–2009). The numbers from 2009 were calculated by the author based on data presented by Araripe (2010).

Contrary to some trends in developed countries, Brazil's newspaper industry has not experienced a dramatic decline in circulation. However, a closer look at the data reveals an important peculiarity. The good performance of the sector is a result of the tabloids' commercial success, rather than an indication of the good health of quality papers. Figure 9.5 presents the share of circulation of the top ten newspapers in Brazil, according to type (quality papers vs. tabloids). The data show a steady growth of tabloids' market share, from 21 per cent in 1996 to 47 per cent in 2009. The increase of circulation from 2005 to 2008 was mostly due to good performance of the popular press, while the circulation of most quality papers has remained relatively stable (Magalhães 2008).

It is important to note that data about newspaper circulation in Brazil do not include publications that are owned by religious groups. The most important example in this regard is the weekly newspaper *Folha Universal*, launched in 1992 by the Universal Church of the Kingdom of God (UCKG). This neo-Pentecostal paper, which prints more than one million copies per week, focuses on news about the Church's activities, but it also covers politicians and public officials affiliated to the Church. UCKG owns several other media outlets, including thirty radio stations, two publishing houses, and a recording studio (Magalhães 2008: 30; Reis 2006: 177).

Key pressures facing the news media

Having summarised the main trends in Brazil's communications landscape, I now turn to the identification of the main constraints that shape the evolution of news organisations. The aim is to discern, albeit in an admittedly incomplete and preliminary fashion, the main challenges and opportunities facing the news media in Brazil. I start with key events that took place in the 1990s.

Bad management and indebtedness

Brazilian news organisations are facing severe economic difficulties, but for different reasons to their counterparts in the USA and other developed nations. The current financial problems of the sector have their roots in the 1990s, especially in the period of Fernando Henrique Cardoso's presidency (1995–2002). Cardoso's administration succeeded in controlling inflation and in stabilising the economy through *Plano Real*, a series of measures that included the introduction of a new currency (real), which initially maintained parity with the US dollar. It was in this context of economic stability and a strong currency that media owners decided to make expensive and questionable investments that would later come back to haunt them. For example, in their traditional push to control or have a strong presence in all sectors of the cultural industries, Globo Organisations launched NET Serviços in 1992, which became the main provider of cable TV in Brazil. However, pay-TV penetration remained stagnant in Brazil (see Figure 9.1) and NET soon accumulated a significant debt. The company defaulted on its obligations in December 2002 and only three years later it was able to announce a restructuring of its US$1.4 billion debt (Benson 2005). Besides the pay-TV market, Globo also invested about $70 million to start the tabloid *Extra* and the news-magazine *Época* in 1998 (Lobato 2004). Several other news organisations initiated expensive projects in the period. It has been estimated that in the second half of the 1990s Brazilian newspapers spent between $600 million and $700 million in the purchase of new printing facilities (Lobato 2004).

These investment decisions became particularly problematic when the economic conditions changed significantly in the beginning of Cardoso's second presidential term. In the first months of 1999 Cardoso's administration put an end to the parity between the real and the US dollar. The Brazilian currency immediately faced a 40 per cent devaluation and in the following years the value of the US dollar climbed from one to four Brazilian reals. Since about 85 per cent of the media groups' debt was in US dollars, the devaluation of the national currency had a devastating impact on the sector. By the early 2000s, the total debt of media companies was estimated to be around $3 billion, with 60 per cent of this debt belonging to the Globo conglomerate (Lins da Silva 2008; Lobato 2004). As several authors note, bad management in a context of shifting economic conditions is a key factor that helps explain the current financial problems of news organisations in Brazil (Correa 2005; Pieranti 2006).

TV Globo's market dominance

As we have seen, broadcast television has absorbed on average more than 59 per cent of all advertising revenues in Brazil. In 2009, the share of the advertising market directed to free-to-air TV achieved a record high of 61 per cent (see Table 9.1). Most of this revenue goes to TV Globo, which grabs between 60 and 75 per cent of all advertising revenues directed to the television sector (Sinclair 2009). The concentration of ownership in the media market and the shrinking share of advertising revenues directed to traditional media (newspapers, news-magazines, and radio) will remain as powerful obstacles to a greater diversification of Brazil's news media.

The key role of socio-economic conditions

The decline of newspaper circulation is not a universal process. In fact, data about newspaper sales around the world suggest that the phenomenon is mostly limited to wealthier nations. Between 2004 and 2008, newspaper circulation declined 9.2 per cent in North America and 2.9 per cent in Europe, but it increased 16.4 per cent in South America, 16.1 per cent in Asia, and 14.2 per cent in Africa (WAN 2009: 2). Developments in Brazil confirm these trends. As we have seen, print media sales improved in Brazil between 2006 and 2008 (see Figure 9.4). Contrary to developed nations, where newspaper circulation tends to decline even during periods of economic prosperity, there is a clear correlation between the performance of the Brazilian economy and the consumption of print media. Several authors have identified a strong linkage between the annual growth rates of Brazil's Gross Domestic Product and the levels of newspaper circulation (Magalhães 2008: 29; Molina 2010; Sant'Anna 2008: 45). Thus, if the Brazilian economy maintains its recent growth trends the prospects for news organisations will improve.

Besides the economy, social conditions also constrain the development of the news media. Levels of poverty, social inequality, and illiteracy have important consequences for information industries. As previously noted, high levels of income concentration help explain the poor performance of new technologies in Brazil, as the case of pay TV demonstrates. However, Brazil's socio-economic context has been characterised by recent improvements in key social indicators. Figures 9.6, 9.7, and 9.8 present data about poverty and illiteracy levels, as well as the evolution of social inequality (as measured by the Gini coefficient). Figure 9.7 shows that there was a significant decline of poverty levels in 1995, the first year of Fernando Henrique Cardoso's presidency, but the proportion of households below the poverty line remained constant during his remaining seven years in office (1996–2002). As Figure 9.8 shows, Cardoso's educational policies had a very positive and consistent performance in the reduction of illiteracy, which declined from 15.9 per cent in 1993 to 10.9 per cent in 2002. As far as social inequality is concerned, income concentration remained high during Cardoso's presidency, with a small decline in his last years in office. On the other hand, all three indicators (poverty, social inequality, and illiteracy) declined significantly during the administration of Luiz Inácio Lula da Silva (2003–10). These changes are a direct consequence of President Lula's social programmes, especially *Bolsa Família*, a conditional cash transfer programme that has benefited roughly 11 million low-income families (Hunter and Power 2007; Soares *et al.*, 2010).

Figure 9.6. Evolution of social inequality in Brazil – Gini Coefficient

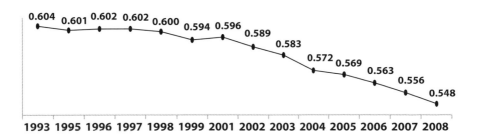

Data from IPEA, http://www.ipeadata.gov.br. Data from 1994 are not available. (Value 0 means no inequality; value 1 means maximum inequality)

Figure 9.7. Proportion of Brazilian households below the poverty line (%)

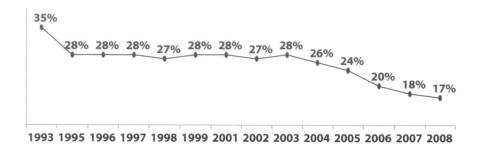

Data from IPEA, http://www.ipeadata.gov.br. Data from 1994 are not available.

Figure 9.8. Evolution of illiteracy in Brazil: % of illiterate citizens (10 years of age or older)

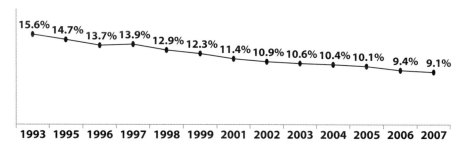

Data from IBGE, http://www.ibge.gov.br. Data from 1994 are not available.

A central argument of this chapter is that changes in Brazil's socio-economic context have had a positive impact on the media system. Recent improvements in household penetration of new technologies, such as pay TV and the internet (see Figure 9.1), are directly linked to a significant reduction of poverty and social inequality. In fact, improvements in the penetration of pay TV since 2005 have been attributed, in part, to new commercial strategies by cable and satellite companies, who started to develop cheaper packages for middle- and low-income families (Goyzueta 2010). On the other hand, the growing commercial success of tabloids (see Figure 9.5) has been linked to the broadening of the reading public with the inclusion of low-income readers who did not choose to buy newspapers before (Araripe 2010). If trends in the reduction of poverty, inequality, and illiteracy continue, news organisations will find new opportunities for growth, with potentially positive consequences for a greater diversification of the media landscape.

What about the internet?

Some scholars argue that the growth of the internet has been one of the main pressures facing news organisations in Brazil. In the case of the newspaper industry, for example, it has been suggested that the World Wide Web played a major role in redirecting readers and advertising investments away from the print media sector (Magalhães 2008;

Sant'Anna 2008). It is hard to know what impact the internet has had on Brazilian news organisations, since there is a lack of systematic research about the topic. Despite the limitations of the available data, this chapter suggests that several other variables have had a more significant impact, including the problematic investment decisions of the 1990s, market concentration by TV Globo, and the broader socio-economic context.

It is important to acknowledge, however, that the Brazilian media landscape is changing rapidly. The recent growth of the internet – which was facilitated, as we have seen, by higher rates of economic growth and the reduction in poverty and social inequality – suggests that the challenges created by the digital revolution have become more significant. Data from 2009 show that one in every four households in Brazil has internet access (see Figure 9.1). Moreover, two-thirds of these households with access have faster, higher quality broadband connection, as opposed to the traditional dial-up technology.[7] Thus, not only has internet penetration become more significant, but the dissemination of faster connections now facilitates access to a greater variety of content, including video streaming. The future of news organisations will depend on how they react to this new landscape.

The internet has opened a new frontier of political blogs and independent content producers. However, it has not yet become a significant sphere for accountability journalism in Brazil. Even those who praise the internet for providing alternative sources of political information to a mostly conservative news establishment acknowledge its limitations. For example, Idelber Avelar (2008), himself an influential blogger, highlights the leading political role that the internet has played in key political moments, but admits that Brazilian cyberspace does not yet come close to the US context, where blogs have played a central role as agents of accountability by developing independent investigations.

Facing the challenges: responses by key actors

Having characterised key pressures facing news organisations in Brazil, this final section considers how key actors have responded to them. I focus on two main actors: policy-makers and media companies.

Responses by policy-makers

When the indebtedness crisis of the media companies erupted in the 1990s, there were two main responses by policy-makers: the opening of the media market to foreign investors and an attempt to provide a massive government loan to news organisations.

Until 2002, Brazilian constitutions had forbidden the entrance of foreign capital into the media sector. But when news organisations faced a severe debt crisis following the devaluation of the real in the late 1990s and early 2000s, media and political actors began considering the possibility of attracting foreign investors to ameliorate the sector's lack of capital. With support of the main media groups, President Fernando Henrique Cardoso and the political parties of his centre-right coalition presented a constitutional amendment to allow the flow of foreign capital to the media sector. Constitutional Amendment 36 was approved by Congress on 28 May 2002, and in the same year Law 10610 regulated the new constitutional provisions. The amendment allows foreigners

---

[7] *Centro de Estudos sobre as Tecnologias da Informação e da Comunicação* (CETIC), www.cetic.br.

and recently naturalised Brazilian citizens to acquire up to 30 per cent of the total capital of news organisations and broadcasting companies (Pieranti 2006: 111). The changes followed the trend started by the 1995 Cable Law (Law 8.977/95), which had already allowed foreign investors to own up to 49 per cent of the capital of cable companies.

Despite the constitutional changes, there was no immediate flow of foreign capital to Brazil's media sector. Only in 2004 did the first major foreign investments take place. In that year, Globopar, the subsidiary that controls cable company NET Serviços, announced a partnership with Telmex, the Mexican telecommunications giant conglomerate owned by Carlos Slim (Lima 2006: 105–7; Pieranti 2006: 115). New foreign investments followed. In May 2005, the Civita family announced the transfer of 30 per cent of group Abril's capital to the South African media company Naspers in a $422 million deal (Lima 2006: 107–8; Sant'Anna 2008: 124). In May 2006, a partnership between TV Globo and Rupert Murdoch's News Corporation launched Sky, a satellite television provider. The Globo group controls 28 per cent of Sky's capital, while News Corporation is in charge of the remaining 72 per cent (Lima 2006: 109). As noted above, the Portuguese conglomerate Ongoing Media Group purchased Grupo O Dia Comunicação in April 2010, in a first major takeover of a newspaper chain by a foreign group. The 2002 constitutional amendment has therefore led to a growing presence of foreign capital in Brazil's media sector.

Another response of policy-makers to the debt crises of the 1990s was an attempt to provide direct government loans to the media. In 2003, media companies requested special loans to BNDES, a state-owned development bank. The request included about $400 million for the purchase of paper and a $1.7 billion credit line to refinance debts (Pieranti 2006: 114). In response, BNDES offered a smaller loan package (about $1.3 billion). However, several sectors of Brazilian society protested against the possibility of a massive government assistance package to the private media, fearing that taxpayers' money would be used to consolidate monopolistic media conglomerates. There was also a widespread fear that media and political elites would engage in clientelistic relations, undermining the independence of the press in relation to the federal government. After much controversy, the media sector announced in July 2004 that it was withdrawing the loan request.

Responses by media companies

Media companies have reacted to the new pressures and opportunities in a variety of ways. Newspapers have taken an active role in adapting to the challenges presented by the internet. In 2008, there were already 133 daily newspapers in Brazil with online editions (WAN 2009: 264). The quality of online journalism, though, is often problematic. An analysis of four of Brazil's main news portals (UOL, Estadão, IG, and Terra) has found that they offer low levels of interactivity and multimedia applications and that their news coverage often lacks depth (Herscovitz 2009).

Taking advantage of a socio-economic context characterised by improvements in the purchasing power of low-income Brazilians, media companies have often invested in popular newspapers to improve sales and revenues. As we have seen, a common strategy of news organisations has been the launching of tabloids, whose commercial success contributed to improving newspaper circulation between 2005 and 2008.

The more complex and challenging communications landscape has led to significant changes in the business model of several news organisations in Brazil. The family groups that control the main quality papers have responded to a context of indebtedness and declining or stagnant circulation by withdrawing from the day-to-day management of their news organisation. For example, the family Marinho, which publishes the newspaper *O Globo*, and the family Mesquita, owner of the newspaper *Estado de S. Paulo*, have given up management positions in their companies, adopting a more corporate-oriented and market-driven administration structure (Sant'Anna 2008: 18–19). Such restructuring has important consequences for news organisations, leading to a business culture that rejects investments that do not provide short-term returns. As a result, news organisations have often eliminated or reduced the number of correspondents and resources required for investigative journalism (Sant'Anna 2008: 18–19). They have also tried to increase profit margins by reducing the size of newsrooms. It has been estimated that between 2001 and 2006 news organisations eliminated about 17,000 jobs (Pieranti 2006: 113). The reform of the newspaper *Folha de S. Paulo* illustrates the new patterns. Contradicting its own reports about improvements in economic conditions and circulation, the paper fired almost 100 journalists in July 2004 (Corrêa 2005: 29).

Brazil's news organisations face contradictory pressures. On the one hand, they have experienced a significant process of modernisation, with higher levels of professionalisation and more balanced patterns of political coverage (Azevedo 2006; Matos 2008; Porto 2007b). On the other hand, they have been affected more recently by the rise of a corporatised and market-driven management structure that favours short-term profits over the quality of news content. The prospects of Brazil's print media sector will depend on how policy-makers, media companies, and other actors respond to these contradictory pressures.

Conclusions: implications for democracy

The changing landscape of the news media in Brazil and the responses of policy-makers and media companies to its challenges have complex consequences to Brazilian democracy. On the one hand, the opening of media markets to foreign investors has not contributed to diversifying the media landscape. Brazilian media corporations have aligned themselves with transnational conglomerates to consolidate their market position, taking advantage of the absence of regulations limiting market concentration. On the other hand, policy-makers' attempt to provide direct loans to media organisations faced strong resistance and ultimately failed.

To solve short-term financial problems, several news organisations in Brazil have adopted a market-driven administration structure and culture. However, recent decisions to cut newsroom budgets and staff will ultimately have negative long-term consequences for news organisations. Studies suggest that the quality of Brazilian journalism has been negatively affected by the recent restructuring of media companies, which in turn has led to a growing dissatisfaction among news consumers (Sant'Anna 2008). The future of journalism in Brazil will depend on the ability of media conglomerates to produce high-quality content.

The tabloidisation of Brazil's print media sector raises important questions about the relationship between media and democracy. However, there is little research about the content and the audience of the growing tabloid press. It is therefore difficult to assess its broader social and political impact. Future research should explore the possibility that these publications contribute to increasing the levels of political information of a mass population that would otherwise not be interested in following politics and public affairs.

Recent trends in Brazilian economy and society have opened new business opportunities to news organisations. The reduction of poverty, social inequality, and illiteracy, as well as improvements in the penetration of new technologies, are some the contextual factors that unleash new prospects for journalism. However, the ability of media companies to fully explore these opportunities will depend on how successful they are in attracting the 'new publics' that have emerged with Brazil's process of democratisation. This will require news organisations to provide more balanced and pluralistic content, while overcoming their traditional elitism by connecting to the aspirations of the new middle- and low-income media consumers. The prospects for journalism will therefore depend on how well they perform in the deepening of democracy in Brazil.

References

Albuquerque, A. d. (2005) 'Another "Fourth Branch": Press and Political Culture in Brazil', *Journalism*, 6/4: 486–504.

Amaral, R., and Guimarães, C. (1994) 'Media Monopoly in Brazil', *Journal of Communication*, 44(4): 26–38.

Araripe, S. (2010) 'Populares são campeões de venda', *Meio & Mensagem* (17 May): 24–7.

Avelar, I. (2008) 'A mídia brasileira na encruzilhada entre o golpismo e a democratização', *Revista UFG*, 10(5): 32–6.

Azevedo, F. (2006) 'Mídia e democracia no Brasil: relações entre o sistema de mídia e o sistema político', *Opinião Pública*, 12(1): 88–113.

Benson, T. (2005) 'Cable Company Reworks Debt', *New York Times* (March 24).

Birman, P., and D. Lehmann (1999) 'Religion and the Media in a Battle for Ideological Hegemony: The Universal Church of the Kingdom of God and TV Globo in Brazil', *Bulletin of Latin American Research*, 18/2: 145–64.

Bolaño, C., and V. Brittos (2008) 'TV pública, políticas de comunicação e democratização: Movimentos conjunturais e mudança estrutural', *Revista de Economia Politicas de las Tecnologias de la Información y Comunicación*, 10/2.

Brittos, V. (2000) 'As Organizações Globo e a reordenação das comunicações', *Intercom: Revista Brasileira de Ciências da Comunicação*, 23/1: 57–76.

Correa, E. (2005) 'Digital Media in Brazil: Crisis or New Identity?', *Brazilian Journalism Research*, 1/2: 25–40.

Duarte, L. (1996) É pagar para ver: A TV por assinatura em foco. São Paulo: Summus.

Goyzueta, V. (2010) 'Todos ligados', *América Economia* (May): 24–7.

Hallin, D., and Papathanassopoulos, S. (2002) 'Political Clientelism and the Media: Southern Europe and Latin America in Comparative Perspective', *Media, Culture and Society*, 24/2: 175–95.

Herscovitz, H. (2009) 'Brazilian News Portals Characteristics', *Brazilian Journalism Research*, 5/1: 99–122.

Hoineff, N. (1996) *A nova televisão*. Rio de Janeiro: Relume Dumará.

Hunter, W., and T. Power (2007) 'Rewarding Lula: Executive Power, Social Policy, and the Brazilian Elections of 2006', *Latin American Politics and Society*, 49/1: 1–30.

Lima, V. (1988) 'The State, Television and Political Power in Brazil', *Critical Studies in Mass Communication,* 5(2): 108–28.

— (2001) *Mídia: Teoria e política.* São Paulo: Editora da Fundação Perseu Abramo.

— (2006) *Mídia: Crise política e poder no Brasil.* São Paulo: Editora Fundação Perseu Abramo.

Lins da Silva, C. E. (2008) 'Television in Brazil', in D. Ward (ed.), *Television and Public Policy.* New York: Lawrence Erlbaum Associates, 27–43.

Lobato, E. (2004) 'Mídia nacional acumula dívida de R$ 10 bilhões', *Folha de S. Paulo* (15 Feb.).

Lotz, A. D. (2007) *The Television will be Revolutionzed.* New York: New York University Press.

Magalhães, L. (2008) 'Jornalismo impresso: Reinvenção ou decadência?', *Revista UFG,* 5/5: 23–36.

Mariano, R. (2004) 'Expansão pentecostal no Brasil: O caso da Igreja Universal', *Estudos Avançados,* 18/52: 121–38.

Matos, C. (2008) *Journalism and Political Democracy in Brazil.* Lanham, Md.: Rowman & Littlefield.

Mira, M. C. (1995) *Circo eletrônico: Silvio Santos e o SBT.* São Paulo: Edições Loyola.

Molina, M. (2010) 'Otimismo apesar da queda', *Valor Econômico* (19 March).

Parente, E. (2009) 'Para onde vai a audiência da TV?', *Meio & Mensagem* (11 May): 35–7.

Pieranti, O. (2006) 'Políticas para a mídia: Dos militares ao governo Lula', *Lua Nova,* 68: 91–121.

Porto, M. (1999) 'Novas tecnologias e política no Brasil: a globalização em uma sociedade periférica e desigual', paper presented at the 21st International Congress of the Latin American Studies Association, Chicago, United States.

— (2003) 'Mass Media and Politics in Democratic Brazil', in M. D. A. Kinzo and J. Dunkerley (eds.), *Brazil since 1985.* London: Institute of Latin American Studies, 288–313.

— (2007a) *Televisão e política no Brasil: A Rede Globo e as interpretações da audiência.* Rio de Janeiro: E-papers.

— (2007b) 'TV News and Political Change in Brazil: The Impact of Democratization on TV Globo's Journalism', *Journalism,* 8/4: 381–402.

Reis, R. (2006) 'Media and Religion in Brazil: The Rise of TV Record and UCKG and their Attempts at Globalization', *Brazilian Journalism Research,* 2/2: 167–82.

Sant'Anna, L. (2008) *O destino do jornal.* Rio de Janeiro: Record.

Santos, S. d., and S. Capparelli (2004) 'Crescei e multiplicai-vos: A explosão religiosa da televisão brasileira', *Intexto,* 2/11: 1–24.

Silva, C. (2010) 'Mercado em movimento', *Meio & Mensagem* (17 May): 4–9.

Sinclair, J. (1999) *Latin American Television.* New York: Oxford University Press.

— (2009) 'The Advertising Industry in Latin America: A Comparative Study', *International Communication Gazette,* 71/8: 713–33.

Soares, F., Ribas, R., and Osório, R. (2010) 'Evaluating the Impact of Brazil's Bolsa Família: Cash Transfer Programs in Comparative Perspective', *Latin American Research Review,* 45/2: 173–90.

Straubhaar, J. (1989) 'Television and Video in the Transition from Military to Civilian Rule in Brazil', *Latin American Research Review,* 24(1): 140–54.

— (1996) 'The Electronic Media in Brazil', in R. Cole (ed.), *Communication in Latin America*. Wilmington, Del.: Scholarly Books, 217–43.

— (2007) *World Television: From Global to Local*. Thousand Oaks, Calif.: Sage.

Turner, G., and J. Tay, eds (2009) *Television Studies After TV: Understanding Television in the Post-Broadcast Era*. London: Routledge.

WAN (2009) *World Press Trends*. Paris: World Association of Newspapers.

Wilkin, P. (2008) 'Global Communication and Political Culture in the Semi-Periphery: The Rise of the Globo Corporation', *Review of International Studies*, 34: 93–113.

10. The Business of 'Bollywoodized' Journalism

Daya Kishan Thussu

Introduction

The business of journalism in India has experienced extraordinary changes in recent years, spurred on by a combination of rapid growth and the globalisation of Indian media industries, as well as technological innovation and convergence which have transformed the media landscape in the world's largest democracy. In contrast to much of the Western world, journalism in India is thriving, as the country records consistent and robust economic growth, rising literacy, and the demonstrable purchasing power of the burgeoning middle class, which is increasingly discovering the pleasures of lifestyle and leisure journalism. In this chapter, I want to examine the state of journalism within this rapidly evolving social and political space as India integrates more fully with the US-dominated global media sphere.

The rapid liberalisation, deregulation, and privatisation of media and cultural industries in India, coupled with the increasing availability of digital delivery and distribution technologies, has created a new market for news vendors. The most striking change is in the broadcast sector: the exponential growth of television channels: from the national broadcaster Doordarshan, a monotonous state monopoly, to more than 400 channels, including seventy dedicated news networks, making it the world's most competitive news market (Thussu 2007a).

When television was introduced in India in 1959 as a means for disseminating government policies and public information, the government-owned channel Doordarshan was used ostensibly to contribute to 'nation-building'. It was not known for providing professional news. News on All India Radio, the state-run radio, had greater reach and credibility but both Doordarshan and All India Radio were accurately perceived as mouthpieces for the government of the day, reflected especially in the unprofessional way their information bureaucrats ran news operations (Mehta 2008). The partial privatisation of the airwaves started with the introduction of advertising by the state broadcaster in the 1970s, followed by sponsored programmes. This received a boost as India opened up to transnational media corporations in the 1990s. The gradual deregulation and privatisation of broadcasting during that decade transformed the industry, making India one of the most lucrative markets for transnational broadcasters (Thussu 2007a, 2007b; Mehta 2008; Kohli-Khandekar 2010).

The Indian authorities were not fully prepared to deal with the technological and multilateral forces that globalisation unleashed – including a multiplicity of television channels. The initial reaction indicated no clear policy framework, allowing private cable and satellite operators to beam programmes imported from the West. Unlike in the field of information technologies, the Indian government's policy response to expansion and deregulation of television demonstrated hesitation and confusion. Indeed, it has been argued that having no coherent policy was itself a policy – at least in the initial period of the appearance of transnational media conglomerates on the Indian broadcasting scene (Thomas 2010). Given the neo-liberal ideological framework that the Indian government had adopted in the 1990s, it was difficult for it to 'ban' Western television, fearing alienating domestic pro-market public opinion and jeopardising much-needed foreign direct investment to fuel economic growth (McDowell 1997). After initial anxiety about the 'invasion' from the sky, Doordarshan started commercialising specific bands of broadcast hours, thus providing domestic private producers opportunities for programming and airtime sales. To remain relevant in a competitive market, it also began to change its content, cutting back on educational and developmental programmes and replacing these with advertising-financed soap operas and infotainment fare (Thomas 2010). After the 1995 ruling by the Supreme Court of India that airwaves were not the 'sole property' of the government, the broadcasting scene witnessed a revolution with a variety of national and transnational cable and satellite operators exploiting the 'choice and diversity' that the ruling ensured.

The policy-makers realised that the government would lose massive revenue from the growing TV distribution sector, prompting the establishment of the Cable Television Networks Regulatory Act 1995 which enabled the government to tax private cable operators, considerably expanding the revenue base of the official broadcaster. In 1998, the government introduced a foreign equity cap of 20 per cent in broadcasting, which was raised subsequently to 100 per cent in the non-news sector, though in the news sector it remains at 26 per cent. Such restrictions of foreign ownership of news networks have arguably not deterred transnational media conglomerates from entering Indian media space as they have consolidated their position in the entertainment arena. By 2009, 461 channels were in operation – forty-four of which were broadcasting in English, making India – a country with 500 million TV viewers – one of the world's largest English-language television markets (FICCI-KPMG 2010).

In contrast to broadcast journalism, newspapers and news-magazines were privately owned and robustly independent. The press was professionally organised and ideologically diverse, and contributed considerably in creating a space for democratic discourse and its sometimes adversarial role acted as an 'early-warning system' for serious food shortages and thus a preventive mechanism against famine (Ram 1990). In parallel with the transformation of the broadcasting sector, there was also a massive expansion in newspaper circulation in the 1990s: particularly prominent are newspapers in Indian languages such as the Hindi-language *Dainik Jagran*, which has emerged as India's largest circulation newspaper (Ninan 2007). Newspapers and news-magazines in other Indian languages, notably Tamil and Telugu, are also growing in circulation, a manifestation of increasing levels of literacy in India as well as greater regionalisation of national political discourse. According to the World Association of

Newspapers, in 2009, India was the world's largest newspaper market with 110 million copies sold every day. The country had 2,337 'paid-for' daily newspapers – the highest number in the world (WAN 2010).

This unprecedented growth – both in broadcasting and print media – has been underpinned by huge increases in advertising revenue as Western-based media conglomerates tap into the growing market of 300 million middle-class Indians with enhanced purchasing power and media-induced aspirations to a consumerist lifestyle (Ganguly-Scrase and Scrase 2008). Cable and satellite television have increased substantially since their introduction in 1992, growing annually at the rate of 10 per cent. The media and entertainment business, one of the fastest growing industries in India, is projected to reach nearly $23 billion by 2011, according to a report prepared by PricewaterhouseCoopers for the Federation of Indian Chamber of Commerce and Industry (FICCI 2007). In India, television takes a large share of advertising revenue: in 2009, TV share of ad-spend was 40 per cent of the total, while 9,400 advertisements were aired in the course of the year, and during primetime slots, 17 minutes in an hour was pure advertising (FICCI-KPMG 2010).

This growth has yet to reach the emerging world of online media, which is still in its infancy. Such communication tools as Twitter, Facebook, YouTube, and MySpace are relatively elitist operations as internet penetration remains limited. According to data from the International Telecommunication Union, only 81 million were internet users – merely 7 per cent of India's 1.2 billion population. Broadband subscription was barely 5.2 million. Even within this small demographic, use of online news is limited. There is little doubt that in the coming decades these apparently free media will challenge the standard models of the business of journalism as generally experienced in the US and Western Europe. Despite the extraordinary growth in online media, 'old' media – radio, newspapers and television – remain by most accounts the premier media, especially in a global context. According to Internet World Stats, by the end of 2009 only 26 per cent of the world's population had access to the internet, and this was skewed in favour of a few developed countries. In the developing world, the internet remains predominantly an elite medium: in Africa just 7 per cent of the population has access, as against nearly 75 per cent in the US (Internet World Stats 2010).

A market-driven news ecology

Conforming to global trends in media systems, it would appear that in India too in the contest between state broadcasting and the private media, the commercial model of broadcast journalism has won, a phenomenon that Hallin and Mancini have characterised as the 'triumph of the liberal model' (2004: 251). Such a media model privileges a commercial model of journalism, where news becomes like any other commodity that needs to be sold in a competitive and crowded news marketplace. This can force journalists to privilege 'soft' news, in which lifestyle and consumer journalism become more prominent, at the expense of public-interest news (Hamilton 2003; Baker 2007).

The trend is well established within the news culture of the United States where broadcasting – both radio and television – had a commercial remit from its very inception, with the trio of networks – CBS (Columbia Broadcasting System), NBC (National Broadcasting Corporation), and ABC (American Broadcasting Corporation) – providing both news and entertainment.

With the creation of a multi-channel broadcasting environment during the 1990s, the three networks started losing audience and advertising revenue. This coincided with the acquisition of key news networks by conglomerates whose primary interest is in the entertainment industry: until recently Viacom-Paramount owned CBS News; ABC News is part of Disney; CNN is a key component of Time-Warner and Fox News is owned by Rupert Murdoch's News Corporation. In addition, the proliferation of news outlets is paralleled by a growing competition for audiences and, crucially, advertising revenue, at a time when interest in news is waning in the US. 'Since 1980 network evening newscasts have lost an average of one million viewers a year,' says the *2010 State of the News Media* report. 'We estimate,' it adds, 'that network news staffs had already been cut by roughly half from their peak in the 1980s' (Pew 2010).

Such a media ecology has required broadcasters and news managers to make journalism more entertaining, often adopting or adapting ideas from the world of entertainment with an emphasis on storytelling and spectacle about celebrities, supplemented by the popular genre of reality TV (Gitlin 2002; Hamilton 2003). This feeds into and benefits from the 24/7 news cycle, thus sustaining ratings and keeping production costs low – a phenomenon replicated among newsrooms around the world (Thussu 2007a).

'Bollywoodized' journalism

Not immune to trends emanating from key centres of global journalism, India has also experienced a new variety of journalism, one which is hostage to infotainment. As newspapers have increased in numbers and reach and television news networks have proliferated, the audience has fragmented on linguistic, cultural, and class lines. Given the diversity of the media – from elite English-language TV news networks, newspapers and news-magazines, to more popular media in languages spoken by a majority of Indians, there is a spectrum of quality, depth, and professionalism. Some of the English-language networks, notably NDTV 24×7 and newspapers such as *The Hindu*, subscribe to the highest professional standards of journalism and are comparable to the best in the world. At the other end of the spectrum, one can place news networks, newspapers, and magazines – many in Hindi – which veer towards a sensationalist editorial agenda. These have much higher circulation figures and attract huge viewership and therefore are crucial in shaping political discourse in a noisy democracy. In 2009, five out of the ten highest circulation newspapers were in Hindi – *The Times of India* was the only English-language daily among the top ten, while the Hindi news channel Aaj Tak was top news network in terms of viewership.

In most cases, in order to survive in a competitive marketplace, journalists are constantly under pressure to lower the threshold of taste and decorum to reach the desired ratings or readerships. Cinema and sport dominate most of the content of Indian newspapers and TV news programmes. Prominent among these is the apparent obsession of almost all news channels and most newspapers, including those representing the high end of the spectrum such as NDTV 24×7, with celebrity culture, which in India centres on Bollywood, the world's largest film factory which is increasingly integrating into a global media sphere, shaped and dominated by the US conglomerates (Kavoori and Punathambekar 2008). The news networks have skilfully adapted Bollywood conventions of melodrama and spectacle, peppered with song-and-dance numbers, to gain new viewers or retain existing ones.

Rupert Murdoch was instrumental in popularising Bollywoodized journalism in India when, in 2000, he used Star News, India's first 24/7 news channel, then part of News Corporation, to promote *Kaun Banega Crorepati*, an Indian version of the British game show *Who Wants to be a Millionaire?*, hosted by the superstar Amitabh Bachchan on his Star Plus channel. Since then Bollywoodized content appears to have colonised the airwaves, with many leading stars hosting their own shows during primetime and promoting synergies by extensive coverage on news channels (Thussu 2007/b).

This Bollywoodization of news is exemplified by the lifestyle segments of news channels such as *Nightout* (on NDTV 24×7) and *After Hours* (on Zee TV) – regularly broadcasting from the glitterati party scene. A recent example of Bollywood taking over the news agenda was to be witnessed in August 2009 when nearly 16 million people watched the finale of the twenty-seven-part reality show *Rakhi Ka Swayamwar* (Rakhi's wedding) featuring Bollywood starlet Rakhi Sawant. The coverage in news media – including in magazines, newspapers and FM radio shows – was extensive: on the final day of the show, Star News, among others, devoted a half-hour programme to the story.

Such Bollywoodized journalism is on the ascent at all news channels, benefiting from corporate synergies. The company that ran the Hindi news channel, Sahara Samay Rashtriya, is also involved in Bollywood film production and operated a film-based channel called 'Filmy'. Zee News is part of one of India's largest infotainment conglomerates, with extensive interests in entertainment industry – apart from general interest Zee Television, it also runs Bollywood oriented Zee Cinema and Zee Music. TV-18, India's leading content provider and broadcaster of business, consumer, and general news, has also made forays into film production with Studio 18.

Most newspapers follow the lead provided by the news networks, with even supposedly serious ones publishing regular glossy supplements based on Bollywoodized content. In what is termed as 'Page 3 journalism' most newspapers routinely cover celebrity stories focusing on the private lives of Bollywood stars (Nayar 2009). The once staid and sober *Times of India* has a particularly important role in promoting this kind of tabloidisation, with its cover page almost every day carrying a prominent celebrity story. One of the few mainstream newspapers which has so far managed to avoid such coverage is *The Hindu*.

The second major obsession of Indian news is with cricket, the most popular sport in India: more than 60 per cent of global broadcasting revenue for cricket emanates from India. It can be argued that television has contributed in drastically altering the traditional game: the five-day test match has been compressed into a four-hour contest – the so-called 20/20 format – and the Indian Premier League (IPL), launched in 2008, has emerged as the richest league for the sport in the world, valued at $4 billion (Burke 2010). Such is the popularity of cricket celebrities that when Mahendra Singh Dhoni, the captain of the Indian cricket team, got married in July 2010, the media outlets went out of their way to provide wall-to-wall coverage, with full-page stories about every possible aspect of the wedding – this despite the fact that the ceremony was conducted in private with close friends and family and without the prying eyes of journalists.

The increasingly enthusiastic participation of Bollywood celebrities in cricket has transformed the sport into an entertainment spectacle for television, receiving primetime coverage on all news networks and dominating newspaper features pages (Chattopadhyay and Subramanian 2010). Three of the eight IPL league teams are majority-owned by prominent Bollywood stars – Shah Rukh Khan (owns Kolkata

Knight Riders, with a brand value of $22 million), Priety Zinta (owns Kings IX Punjab), and Shilpa Shetty (owns Rajasthan Royals, the team which won the inaugural championship in 2008). Taking a leaf from the lucrative US baseball league matches, the entertainment experience of 20/20 tournaments is 'enhanced' by the presence of dancing cheerleader girls at key points of the game as well as by appearances by Bollywood stars.

'The Indian television news industry', notes a recent study, 'has consciously ridden on the shoulders of cricket' (Mehta 2008: 197). The nexus between Bollywoodized journalism and increasingly corporatised sport has generated a great deal of controversy in the media itself. Allegations of 'match-fixing' and tax evasion by politicians and industrialists who hold shares in IPL have sullied the reputation of the sport. As one commentator wryly noted: 'With the IPL comes the convergence of the most important media trends: the ABC of Media – Advertising, Bollywood and Corporate Power' (Sainath 2010a). It is not surprising then that in 2010 Dhoni was India's most expensive sportsman, promoting a record twenty-two corporate brands.

Pressures on professionalism

As elsewhere in the world, in India ratings-driven television news and circulation wars among competing newspapers are forcing journalists and news executives to go for the safety of the soft news option. The fiercely competitive media market has contributed to a dilution of professional attitudes to journalism – in a country where newspaper journalism has a long and distinguished history with a tradition of investigative journalism and watchdog functions.

One recent example of compromising professionalism was the manner in which many journalists covered the terrorist attacks in Mumbai on 26 November 2008 and the subsequent sixty-hour drama of hostage-taking horror, unfolding live on national television. As competing news networks vied with each other to provide the most sensational and dramatic reportage from India's commercial capital, the atrocity was transformed into a round-the-clock Bollywood thriller. The compulsion of 'breaking news' encouraged some networks to unwittingly provide live telecast of commandos of India's elite National Security Guard being airdropped, potentially endangering the lives of both hostages and security forces.

News networks as well as newspaper columns discussed in detail how Bollywood bloggers such as superstar Amitabh Bachchan posted his reflections on the attacks and their aftermath. One indication of the Bollywoodization of the coverage was that, even before the tragedy – which claimed 166 lives and injured hundreds of Indian and foreign citizens – was over, reports were circulating of producers registering names, such as '26/11: Mumbai under Terror' and 'Operation Five Star Mumbai', for action thrillers based on the macabre events. In a report just weeks after 26/11, a parliamentary panel called for greater regulation of real-time broadcasts during such emergencies while the News Broadcasters Association – a leading professional body of news organisations – set up a self-regulatory 'emergency protocol' for covering terrorism. However, it is likely that commercial imperatives will still dictate what gets on air.

Implications of Bollywoodized journalism for democracy

A more recent and disturbing trend has further eroded the professional credibility of journalism in India: the phenomenon of 'paid news'. This was witnessed during the provincial elections in October 2009 in the western state of Maharashtra (of which Mumbai is the capital), when the Chief Minister Ashokrao Chavan bought editorial space in three leading Marathi-language newspapers to promote his election prospects (Sainath 2009). One commentator did not mince words: 'Whether the Indian media likes to admit it or not, journalism is up for sale' (Raman 2009). The Editors Guild of India strongly condemned the practice, suggesting that it 'whittles down the foundations of Indian journalism' (quoted in Joshua 2009), while the Press Council of India noted: 'The phenomenon of 'paid news' goes beyond the corruption of individual journalists and media companies. It has become pervasive, structured and highly organised and in the process, is undermining democracy in India' (quoted in Sainath 2010b).

It can be argued that, by overwhelming public discourse with Bollywoodized content, national and transnational media conglomerates are debasing the quality of public debate in India, at a time when as a rising power the country is integrating with the US-led neo-liberal economic system, both as a producer and consumer of commodity capitalism. As I have discussed elsewhere, an infotainment-driven journalism has been very successful globally: in Italy, such journalism catapulted Silvio Berlusconi from a businessman to the office of the Prime Minister. In the former Soviet Union, the market has vigorously replaced Marx, while in the Chinese version of capitalism, infotainment works as a powerful ideological trope: the mandarin-language Phoenix channel regularly runs such soft news programmes as *Easy Time, Easy News* (Thussu 2007a).

Has the ascendance of Bollywoodized journalism lulled the capacity for critical engagement with political processes, replacing them with newly acquired consumer fetishism? Is Bollywoodized journalism creating a media culture in which neo-liberalism can take deep roots? Already, the United States, the fount of global commercialised media, is increasingly acquiring acceptance as the favoured model to follow, despite the economic downturn triggered in 2007. A 2009 survey by the Pew Global Attitudes Project found that the US image was very strong in India, with 76 per cent of Indians expressing a positive opinion of the United States, compared with 54 per cent in 2002 (Pew 2009). This admiration for Americana and its locally cloned celebrity culture has ensured that the 'public' aspects of India's social reality have been taken over by private corporate interests, which thrive on what has been called 'celebrity ecology' (Nayar 2009: 181).

This trend to infotainment and celebrity-cricket-centred news has an ideological dimension in a country where, despite impressive economic growth, more than 300 million people remain illiterate. Some have argued that the proliferation of news networks and the freedom from government control has widened and democratised public discourse, as broadcast journalists have helped give voice to the voiceless and seek accountability from political actors (Rao 2008). There is no doubt that a multiplicity of media outlets have helped the citizens to access a wider range of information and analysis. This has also curtailed government's power to control and manage information and thus influence the news agenda. Networks such as NDTV 24×7 have taken up causes in public interest – such as environmental protection, freedom of information, gender inequality – thus forcing government to amend or initiate policy. However, such spirited journalistic interventions are few and far between. For most of the mainstream media such themes do not translate into ratings or circulation figures for urban, Westernised viewers and readers. It is prudent for their news-managers and marketing executives to encourage journalists to displace developmental issues with the diversion of Bollywood-driven infotainment.

Bollywoodized journalism beyond borders

Given the size and scale of the transformation of journalism in India, coupled with the growing involvement of transnational media conglomerates in what is one of the fastest growing economies on the planet, what is happening to journalism in India acquires international significance. As cross-media ownership rules are relaxed, Western investment is increasing in India's media sector. Conversely, Indian media companies are investing outside the national territories, as a recent report noted: 'Aspirations of Indian players to go global and foreign players entering the industry are likely to help the industry target a double digit growth in next five years' (FICCI-KPMG 2010: 15).

As India integrates further into a globalised free-market economy, the Indian version of journalism is likely to have a transnational reach, attracting new viewers, listeners, and readers beyond their traditional South Asian diasporic constituency. The availability of new delivery and distribution mechanisms, as well as the growing corporatisation of its film factories and television and online industry, will ensure that Indian journalism can enter the global media sphere. One key factor is demographic: more than 70 per cent of Indians are below the age of 30 and a sizeable segment of these is increasingly mobile, harnessing the journalistic opportunities offered by the globalisation of media industries and especially using their skills in the English language, the vehicle for global communication. They have successfully made use of this demographic, benefiting at the same time from the growing geopolitical and economic convergence between the governments of India and the United States. It is not a coincidence that two of the leading global news outlets – *Newsweek International* (Fareed Zakaria) and *Washington Post* (Raju Narisetti – Managing Editor) have editors with Indian roots.

News networks have fruitfully deployed the emerging synergies between Bollywood and mainly US-based media transnational corporations. Already, international news organisations, such as CNN have entered into partnerships with Indian companies. CNN-IBN, an English news and current affairs channel, launched in 2005, in association with TV-18 Group, while NDTV Group has strategic ties with NBC, and for two years, 2006–8, Times Now, owned by the *Times of India* Group, ran a joint news operation with Reuters.

In addition, the 24-million strong Indian diaspora increasingly contributes to and benefits from Indian economic growth. The annual contribution to the Indian economy from the Indian diaspora is valued at up to $10 billion. Members of this group are tuning into Indian news channels and accessing online news portals to keep abreast of developments. NDTV 24×7, for example, was available in 2010 to the Indian diaspora in the US (via DirecTV), the UK (BSkyB), the Middle East (Arab Digital Distribution) and southern Africa (Multi-choice Africa).

This global dimension could strengthen the strong democratic tradition within India. Indians take pride in their democracy and the freedom of creative expression that their polity has ensured since independence from Britain in 1947. As a vibrant democracy, the notion of a free flow of information and freedom of expression is deeply entrenched in India. However, freedom of information and expression should come with a high dose of social responsibility, particularly relevant in a nation where the largest number of the world's destitute live – despite huge progress in many areas, including unprecedented growth in the media industry.

For a balanced dynamic to emerge between the freedom to report and social responsibility, there is a pressing need for an autonomous national regulator. The Indian government has been toying with such an idea for nearly two decades now and, despite promises, nothing concrete has been done. In the absence of a professional and credible content regulator, competitive commercial interests have pushed the envelope further in the process of creating their media empires, while debasing public discourse by Bollywoodizing journalism.

References

Baker, C. E. (2007) *Media Concentration and Democracy: Why Ownership Matters*. Cambridge: Cambridge University Press.

Burke, J. (2010) 'Not Just Cricket – Bollywood Treatment Gives India its Very own "Superbowling"', *Guardian* (10 March).

Chattopadhyay, D. and A. Subramanian (2010) 'SRK Inc.', *Business Today* (2 March).

FICCI (2007) *Indian Entertainment and Media Industry: A Growth Story Unfolds*. Mumbai: Federation of Indian Chambers of Commerce and Industry in association with Pricewaterhouse.

FICCI-KPMG (2010) *Back in the Spotlight: FICCI-KPMG Indian Media and Entertainment Report, 2010*. Mumbai: Federation of Indian Chambers of Commerce and Industry.

Ganguly-Scrase, R. and T. Scrase (2008) *Globalization and the Middle Classes in India: The Social and Cultural Impact of Neoliberal Reforms*. London: Routledge.

Gitlin, Todd (2002) *Media Unlimited: How the Torrents of Images and Sounds Overwhelms our Lives*. New York: Metropolitan Books.

Hallin, D. and P. Mancini (2004) *Comparing Media Systems*. Cambridge: Cambridge University Press.

Hamilton, J. (2003) *All the News that's Fit to Sell: How the Market Transforms Information into News*. Princeton: Princeton University Press.

Joshua, A. (2009) 'Editors Guild Denounces Practice of "Paid News"', *The Hindu* (23 Dec.).

Kavoori, A. and A. Punathambekar, eds (2008) *Global Bollywood*. New York: New York University Press.

Kohli-Khandekar, V. (2010) *The Indian Media Business*, 3rd edn. New Delhi: Sage.

McDowell, S. (1997) 'Globalization and Policy Choice: Television and Audiovisual Service Policies in India', *Media, Culture and Society*, 19/2: 151–72.

Mehta, N. (2008) *India on Television: How Satellite News Channels have Changed the Way we Think and Act*. New Delhi: Harper Collins.

Nayar, P. (2009) *Seeing Stars: Spectacle, Society and Celebrity Culture*. New Delhi: Sage.

Ninan, S. (2007) *Headlines from the Heartland: Reinventing the Hindi Public Sphere*. New Delhi: Sage.

Pew Research Center (2009) *Confidence in Obama Lifts US Image around the World Most Muslim Publics Not So Easily Moved*. Pew Global Attitudes Project, Pew

Research Center for the People and the Press, Washington, DC, released 23 July: http://pewglobal.org/reports/display.php?ReportID=264.

— (2010) *The State of the News Media: An Annual Report on American Journalism, 2010*. Journalism.org. http://stateofthemedia.org/2010.

Ram, N. (1990) 'An Independent Press and Anti-Hunger Strategies: The Indian Experience', in J. Dreze and A. Sen (eds), *The Political Economy of Hunger*. Oxford: Clarendon Press, vol. i.

Raman, A. (2009) 'Paid-for news: News you can Abuse', *Outlook* (21 Dec.).

Rao, S. (2008) 'Accountability, Democracy and Globalization: A Study of Broadcast Journalism in India', *Asian Journal of Communication*, 18/3: 193–206.

Sainath, P. (2009) 'Mass Media: Masses of Money?', *The Hindu* (30 Nov.).

— (2010a) 'How to Feed your Billionaires', *The Hindu* (17 April).

— (2010b) 'Paid News Undermining Democracy: Press Council Report', *The Hindu* (21 April).

Thomas, P. (2010) *The Political Economy of Communications in India: The Good, the Bad and the Ugly*. New Delhi: Sage.

Thussu, D. K. (2007a) *News as Entertainment: The Rise of Global Infotainment*. London: Sage.

— (2007b) 'The "Murdochization" of News? The Case of Star TV in India', *Media, Culture and Society*, 29/3: 593–611.

WAN (2010) *World Press Trends: Advertising Revenues to Increase, Circulation Relatively Stable*. World Association of Newspapers: www.wan-press.org/article18612.html (accessed Aug. 2010).

11. Which Way for the Business of Journalism?

Rasmus Kleis Nielsen and David A. L. Levy

Introduction

The business of journalism is changing around the world, faced with cyclical, technological, and long-term challenges. While change is a constant, its character and consequences are variable – across media, across industries, and across borders. Many commercial legacy news organisations face comparable external pressures to their business models, deriving partly from the rise of the internet and partly from the global recession. But even within the developed world of wealthy post-industrial democracies, they face them in different circumstances, operating within different institutional and economic frameworks, subject to different forms of media regulation, and catering to populations with different media habits and demographic profiles.

In some countries, like the United States, the business of journalism is facing what is arguably the greatest crisis in recent history. In other countries the problems generally seem much more limited so far – confined variously to strategic challenges for newspaper publishers, political changes unravelling a previously established media policy consensus, or institutional dysfunctions revealing the shortcomings of inherited arrangements for production and distribution More ominously, some see signs of a crisis of trust in journalism (Coleman *et al.* 2009; Jones 2004), or indeed crisis in the very profession itself (Bennett *et al.* 2007; Barnett 2002). While all these developments today play out alongside a transition to a new and increasingly convergent communications environment, it is important to keep in mind that many of the problems predate both the internet and the recession.

Take as examples Germany, the largest media market in Europe, and the often-discussed case of the United States. In both countries, a highly regionalised newspaper business, historically often based on local monopolies, is increasingly forced to contend with new competitors and faces a structural and market adjustment even as the practice of journalism is changed by a much faster news cycle pulsating across many platforms and powered by ubiquitous computing, mobile communications, and the relative ease of sharing, combining, and modifying digitised data. Both German and American newspapers have had their advertising revenue streams diluted by the vastly increased number of alternative outlets available, and whether one operates out of Cologne in Nordrhein-Westfalen or Charlotte in North Carolina, the financial crisis, housing slump, and all-round recession of 2007–10 has hurt the bottom line.

But German papers generally have more robust and diverse revenue streams than their American counterparts, based as they are less on advertising and more on high numbers of loyal subscribers and increasingly a whole slew of additional services and products sold via each newspaper's brand and privileged relation to its core clientele (book clubs, branded merchandise, events, etc.). German papers also often have more room for manoeuvre – whether they use it or not – than many of their American counterparts as they are generally privately held rather than publicly traded, and thus not forced to orient themselves primarily towards delivering short-term profits.

Such differences have real consequences not only for how the business of journalism is pursued, but also for how journalism is practised, and for what role it can play in democracy. These differences are vividly illustrated as many German papers focus on professionally produced quality content as their potential competitive advantage in a more cut-throat convergent market for advertising revenue and audience attention (where the standard is in part set by national and regional public service media organisations), whereas many chain-owned American newspapers have tried to cut their way to profitability, with the risk that they have reduced their own product to an undifferentiated commodity in a generously supplied market. From 2000 to 2009, the number of journalists employed by German newspapers fell somewhat, from 15,300 to 14,300 (-8 per cent), whereas the US number shrank from 56,200 to 41,500 (-26 per cent) (data on Germany from Esser and Brüggeman in this volume, on the US from Pew 2010). And yet, even without a round of ruthless downsizing, most of the German press seems to have made a healthy profit even in the *annus horribilis* of 2009, when tumbling advertising revenues (a decline of more than $10 billion, or 26 per cent, in one year) pushed a number of newspaper companies in the United States to the brink of bankruptcy – and some into it.

A profitable business today is no guarantee of good journalism, or for a profitable business tomorrow. But as Frank Esser and Michael Brüggemann have demonstrated in their contribution to this book, it seems exaggerated – internet or no internet, recession or no recession – to talk of a crisis in the German business of journalism. The situation in the United States, in contrast, remains grave – if probably not life-threatening for the industry as such. Many indicators have stabilised in 2010 after the precipitous declines of 2007–9, earnings have increased, and operating profits are back in some companies – 'flat is the new up', as the saying goes. But even in the United States, hardest hit of all by the current convulsions in the industry, commercial legacy news organisations are likely to continue to play a central, if both in absolute and relative terms probably diminished, role in a wider convergent communications environment.[1]

---

[1] For historical parallels, think of the film industry, originally based exclusively around cinema box office sales (which declined by 30% in the USA between 1945 and 1955 as television spread, see Bakker 2010), or the music industry, in the late 1990s primarily based on CD sales (the recording industry's revenue declined by 57% between 1999 and 2009 as on-line file-sharing spread, see Goldman 2010). Both industries have undergone painful transitions when forced to contend with new technologies, and have, relatively speaking, shrunk. But they still continue to be important parts of our overall communications environment.

The continuing relevance of commercial legacy news organisations

Even though our communications environment in its entirety has expanded at a much faster pace than the production of content by professional journalists – with the popularisation of online self-expression though blogs, social networks, and content-sharing sites – commercial legacy news organisations in many countries today benefit from similar trends to reach larger audiences than ever before. A number of individual news organisations and media conglomerates particularly exposed to shifts in advertising revenues and new forms of competition, particularly inept in their transition to a new environment, or particularly weighed down by legacy costs, may well collapse as they struggle to capitalise on this audience and fail to prove their relevance and trustworthiness to a new generation. Such are the vagaries of the marketplace and the consequences of rapid change. But where there are pressures the business of journalism as such seems to be in a state of painful transition rather than in a terminal decline. It is not only in emerging markets like Brazil and India – where double-digit economic growth and increased demand from an emerging urban middle class fuels a rapid expansion of the media and entertainment sector   but also in many developed democracies with mature markets – even in countries like Germany and Finland with strong public service providers and high internet penetration – that the business of journalism has a future. Money is being made in parts of the news industry, reporters are paid as they work for it, and people in positions of power – whether in political organisations, civil society associations, or private companies – still worry about how they are covered by professional journalists.

Though we have few doubts about the survival of the business of journalism as such, and see many examples of new and profitable business opportunities opening up both in developed democracies and emerging economies, a reduced but stable (or even thriving) news industry does not automatically produce good journalism, let alone the kinds of journalism desirable in democracies. Operating profits may be a necessary condition for a strong and relatively autonomous commercially funded journalism that can hold the powerful to account, make information available to citizens, and help them navigate the complexities of the contemporary world. But profits are not sufficient. Many news organisations have been as journalistically and democratically undistinguished as they have been profitable for much of the twentieth century. It was, as Clay Shirky (2009) and Michael Schudson (2010) have argued, only through a 'happy accident' combining private profitability, journalistic professionalism, and an organised struggle for a more egalitarian political culture and for transparency in government and business that the commercial press in the United States came to play its imperfect but important role for American democracy. Such contingent compromises have developed in more or less desirable ways in all the countries we discuss, as they have around the world, mixing commercial imperatives, journalistic priorities, and political considerations in different ways. And as many countries see some of these strands unravel in the face of new challenges – whether cyclical, technological, or more long-term – there is cause for concern, and a need for rethinking of business strategies, professional practices, and public policies.

Making the most of a time of change

The different consequences of comparable challenges are rooted in inherited institutions, infrastructures, and habits developed over time, and on time-honed business strategies, professional practices, and political compromises that might work loose or be reformed, but are rarely radically reimagined. Even in times of otherwise profound change, innovation in most cases seems to happen at the margins of the business of journalism (as it has historically) amongst young entrepreneurs, disgruntled professionals, minorities dissatisfied with prevailing norms, alternative media ventures, and so on.

We have little doubt that, where it finds itself in a crisis, the business of journalism must first and foremost rescue itself if it is to be rescued. This calls for both managers ('the business') and journalists ('of journalism') to think more about the road ahead than lament about what has been or what might have been lost. Journalism was arguably never as good as the eulogists claim it was (and rarely as bad as its critics said). What is needed is not necessarily a *replacement* of the paradigmatic business or organisational forms of the twentieth century, but *renewal*, a news industry and a profession ready for the twenty-first century.

Faced with the challenge of renewing their industry, managers understandably worry about profits. But if the news business is to shake the notion that it is predominantly a sunset industry ripe for asset stripping, they will have to worry not only about next quarter's profits, or even next year's, but also about the medium- and long-term prospects. Some privately held companies seem to have a better track record in this regard (An *et al.* 2006) but equally some of those organisations that have seen themselves as best protected from market pressures have sometimes found it hardest to embrace necessary change.[2] Amongst those who do think ahead, the debate seems to circle around attempts to charge more for content across different platforms (pay walls, applications for mobile devices, subscription services, premium membership arrangements, etc.) and around attempts to integrate the business and the professional content it underwrites more with the vastly bigger universe of 'user-generated content' on the internet, to make the news more relevant, and to profit from larger audiences for advertising (the commercial motives behind calls for 'mutualisation': Rusbridger 2009). Clearly, increased exclusivity and increased engagement have quite different democratic implications, in particular in terms of people's access to timely information about current affairs and matters of public importance.

Faced with the challenge of reinventing their vocation, journalists understandably worry about their jobs. But for the profession to reassert its relevance takes more than safe employment and nostalgic talk about often mythical golden ages. Those who are willing to take seriously the claim that 'there has never been a better time to be a journalist' – made in many countries and at many conferences today – face the challenges of leveraging the considerable promise of new information and communication technologies for more informative, engaging, and timely forms of journalism, of re-establishing the profession's connection to all too often lukewarm or even distrustful audiences, and of demonstrating what the added value of professionally produced content is in a new communications environment. Given that there is today a vast amount of *stuff* available at any moment on any conceivable platform, the key challenge is why people – both as consumers and citizens – should pay attention to and

---

[2] Arguably in France while *Le Monde*'s system of collective ownership may have reinforced its editorial independence, it has also made its economic problems harder to address.

perhaps pay for *journalism*?

Though we believe – and hope – that managers and journalists will play a central role in reimagining the business of journalism during a time of change, the business of journalism is too important to leave to media managers and journalists alone. Its future is about more than profit and jobs. It is also about democracy.

Policy-makers – and the citizens they represent or claim to represent – therefore need to think about the business of journalism too. This is the time to do it, a time where we can make what the American sociologist and public policy scholar Paul Starr calls 'constitutive choices', choices that will form our media systems for years to come, and they are not simply managerial choices or professional choices, but also political choices. The business of journalism has always been tightly intertwined with public policy, even in countries like the United States, where direct subsidies have rarely been provided (Starr 2004). Even when not propping up whole industries, governments have with greater or lesser success had to structure media regulation to constitute meaningful markets, protect against the dangers of monopoly, encourage innovation, and ensure provision of content, in terms of its quality, quantity, diversity, and distribution.

As with many areas of public policy, change has often been gradual, characterised more by what political scientists call 'layering' and 'drift' than by deliberate 'conversions' or 'revisions' aimed at establishing new coherent frameworks (Thelen 1999; Hacker 2004). Though media reform movements around the world have called for policy-makers to make the most of this moment of crisis and fundamentally rethink media policy and regulation from a democratic perspective (Pickard *et al.* 2009), we have yet to see many bold new departures from the inherited agendas and policy toolkits, and much media policy continues to be tied to increasingly obsolete notions of platform-specificity (most importantly distinctions between print and broadcast), despite the clear trends towards convergence.

Walking backwards towards an uncertain future?

Conversations about the role public policy should play in shaping the future of journalism have often seemed eminently path-dependent, even in the face of what are in some respects dramatically new situations. Well-known ideological disagreements and inherited national media policy traditions and policy toolkits dominate these debates, and are rarely combined with systematic discussions of ideas from or developments in other countries. From the many examples presented in this book consider briefly the three cases of Germany, the United States, and France.

Most of the German debate revolves around two old issues and one new issue. First of all, the German Newspaper Publishers' Association (BDZ) has made clear that it would like to see anti-trust regulation and cross-media ownership regulation loosened. Secondly, the Private Broadcasters Association (VPRT) has reiterated its call for a roll-back of public service media organisations' quasi-commercial activities, particularly online. Thirdly, industry organisations have called for increased regulation of the use of copyrighted content on the internet, potentially in the form of license fees to be paid by commercial online services (something the German government is pushing for at the European level too).

Much of this conversation has a familiar ring to it. Large newspaper conglomerates have criticised the regulatory framework as too constricting since it was introduced in 1976, and there has been ongoing debate over the unclear nature of public service remits in Germany since the 1970s, driven in particular by industry associations, and increasingly arbitrated by European Union authorities.

Proposals aired in the United States today include suggestions that, first, newspapers might be offered certain tax advantages if they convert to non-profit status, secondly, they should get temporary tax relief, limited antitrust exemption, and that cross-media ownership regulations should be loosened, and, third, that fair use and intellectual property legislation should be changed to make it easier for newspapers to charge content aggregators, search engines, and others who use their content online.

As in Germany, reactions in the US are familiar from previous decades. The non-profit idea has elicited little interest from what is a very large and was until recently a very profitable for-profit industry. It has also run into opposition from some journalists, who believe that the requirement for conversion to non-profit status – including that newspapers stop endorsing candidates in editorials – is a slippery slope that will lead to government regulation of content and thus potentially undermine established First Amendment freedom of the press principles. The second set of measures discussed is easily recognisable as a standard industry position, in particular in times of crisis, and in line with the deregulatory trust of previous legislation like the 1970 Newspaper Preservation Act and the 1996 Telecommunications Act. Discussions of intellectual property are relatively recent arrivals to this policy agenda, but similar in that their orientation often seems more focused on protecting incumbents from the competitive pressure posed by new entrants than on encouraging the business of journalism to transition towards the future.

If German and American journalists and media managers prefer to think they can keep the state out of the business, French journalists and news media seem to prefer to keep it in. In France, the États Généraux de la Presse Écrite launched in 2008 not only discussed, but soon after saw implemented as government policy, first, additional direct subsidies for the printed press, second, tax breaks on delivery services, and, third, a temporary extraordinary shift in government advertising towards the printed press to help it ride out the recession. (In addition, in a pioneering move that some political parties around Europe have declared that they hope to emulate, the state and the industry split the bill for offering every 18–24 year old in the country a subscription to a print publication of their choice.[3])

What the French government did *not* do was break with a long tradition of reacting in just these ways to bail out a permanently troubled and occasionally apparently mortally endangered industry (as had been done most recently in 1995 and 1997) or heed the calls for reform of the system of distribution and production that many analysts argue is at the dysfunctional heart of the French newspaper industry's chronic difficulties. Like their American counterparts, the French conversations gravitated towards discussions of how the existing incumbents could be bailed out by offering increased subsidies and, despite strong criticism from many sides, drifted away from addressing institutional problems, new issues of intellectual property rights and fair use online, and the question of whether existing state subsidies could be given in a manner more conducive for a transition towards the future than a propping up of legacy players.

---

[3] The free subscription is for one issue a week. It is too early to see the results of this scheme as it is only entering its second year. However, an earlier experiment of this kind, launched by 40 regional papers in 2006 (without government support) showed that in the case of the leading regional paper, *Ouest France*, 65% of the young people who took up the offer continued to read the paper once a week thereafter, but only 12% took up a daily paid subscription (AFP 2009).

In all three countries, different as they are in other respects, much of the conversation centres on issues that have been on the agenda from the 1970s and onwards. What kind of regulation can ensure sound business conditions that allow successful companies to leverage economies of scale without at the same time letting consolidation (in particular through mergers and acquisitions) lead to dangerous levels of market concentration and media monopoly? Should state subsidies be introduced for newspapers? What is the best balance between an effective provision of public service and an efficient and self-sustaining market provision of news, current affairs, documentaries, entertainment? And so on.

Calls for policies that go beyond the usual toolkit in these areas have routinely been either rejected or ignored. In both Germany and the United States, calls for direct subsidies, however modest and insulated from government control, have been roundly dismissed by industry associations, journalists, and politicians In France, calls for reform of the institutional framework for printing and distribution built in the immediate post-war years have been met by little more than vague declarations of intent. There are also some striking similarities not only over time, as national debates return to the same points and proposals again and again, but also between countries; for example, between Germany and the United States, where a core part of the conversation concerns similar questions of antitrust and ownership regulation, though the business situation in the two countries in many ways could hardly be any more different. The industry is doing rather well in Germany today, whereas it seems in rather dire straits in the United States.

In the United Kingdom, the policy debate wavers between addressing the dangers posed by the apparent fragility of some commercial news providers and what is seen by some as the excessive strength of the BBC. Local news is seen as the area of greatest vulnerability in the current transition period with, as John Lloyd points out in his chapter, predictions from some that half of the newspaper titles will close over the next five years. Concerns about local newspapers have been accompanied by those about local TV news as the main commercial broadcaster, ITV, cut back on its local news operations (citing declining advertising revenues). Both concerns played into the wider debate about the size and scope of the BBC's activities. Local newspapers – joined by national companies – complained that the BBC's active online sites and proposed local TV service would crowd out their attempts to build a multimedia strategy. Meanwhile the pressures on ITV's local news provision – and reductions in what commercial TV operations spend on news, current affairs, and children's programming – prompted the regulator Ofcom to launch a wider debate about the threat to the UK system of a plurality of public service providers (Gardam and Levy 2008).

The policy responses to these threats have varied. BBC management cancelled its plans for a local TV service after its governing body, the BBC Trust, refused these in the face of commercial complaints. The previous Labour government took up Ofcom's proposals for new forms of local multimedia news organisations supported by a contestable fund from the BBC licence fee, to which new and legacy providers could bid for funding. That proposal has been cancelled by the Conservative-Liberal Democrat government which came into power in May 2010. The coalition government believes there are commercial solutions to fill the future gap in local news provision. The interim report on local TV news published in September 2010, along with subsequent speeches by the Culture Secretary Jeremy Hunt, suggests that future plans will include incentives for partnerships with existing players and a relaxation of cross-media ownership provisions at the local level.

But in spite of these changes, the dominant strand of UK media policy debate has remained relatively constant over at least the past decade, revolving around the right balance between a BBC – which dominates both the news agenda and the use of news online – and existing commercial providers who argue that what the BBC sees as its need to remain relevant to *its* audiences could compromise *their* future. At the level of principle this debate is about the balance in UK media policy between private and public provision or the market versus subsidy. Debates over principle however quickly become personalised as these issues are often portrayed as the incumbent government choosing where to position themselves between Rupert Murdoch's News International and the BBC.[4]

Subsidies, regulation, and the role of public service providers are decades-old issues discussed under changing circumstances. Today, even as these issues rise up the agenda, they are increasingly supplemented with a set of new questions concerning the status of online-only actors, what kind of intellectual property regime is suitable in a new environment, and to what extent new advances in, for example, behavioural targeting and personal profiling conflict with existing norms and legislation (OECD 2010).

In Germany, a large group of publishing organisations, including the market-leading Axel Springer company, have publicised the 'Hamburg Declaration', arguing that 'universal access to our services should be available [online], but going forward we no longer wish to be forced to give away property without having granted permission' (Axel Springer 2010). These German publishers want the right to pre-approve use of their copyrighted content by search engines, news aggregators, and other commercial online operators to be legally enshrined. Their position has received support from the World Association of Newspaper and News Publishers and others. Google and other search engine companies, on the other hand, have argued that existing technical measures such as what is called 'Robots Exclusion Protocol' (REP) allows sufficient control for publishers over their content, and have offered to work with the news industry on developing its online business practices.

In the United States, parallel discussions over online copyright and content have played out around the so-called 'hot news' doctrine and its role in the current communications environment.[5] In reaction to a lawsuit making its way through the American legal system, a who's-who of commercial legacy news organisations (including the Associated Press, the Gannett Company, the New York Times Company, but also Agence France Presse and several others) have argued that if everyone is permitted to systematically appropriate content produced by others, for-profit companies will be deterred from entering or remaining in the news business. Google and Twitter, on the other hand, have argued that it is in the public interest that facts, even when they are originally published by a limited number of influential news organisations, can be republished and broadcast by others. (In both these cases, the

---

[4] See the speeches by James Murdoch (2009) of BSkyB and Mark Thompson (2010) of the BBC at the Edinburgh TV Festivals of 2009 and 2010 respectively.

[5] The doctrine originates in a 1918 Supreme Court Decision upholding on the one hand that there is no copyright in facts, but also suggesting that the economic interests of particular news-gathering organizations should be protected against 'unfair competition' by recognizing that they have a limited proprietary interest in the news they publish, not *vis-à-vis* the public at large, but against competitors profiting from republishing it as their own – the case arose from an Associated Press lawsuit against the competing International News Service, which rewrote AP news and distributed them to subscribers by telegraph.

question of what the commercial half-life of news is remains unanswered. Thomson Reuters CEO Tom Glocer has argued that the answer is 'milliseconds' (quoted by Jarvis 2009) but the answer for general-interest news and long-form journalism may well be quite different from financial news.)

In France, a new law has created an official category of 'online news provider' that applies to the websites of legacy organisations, but also to so-called pure players, thereby giving those who publish original and independent news content equal rights to various forms of indirect and direct state aid – though most of this aid continues to be tied to existing forms of production and distribution. (An estimated €20 million of a total of €600 million in the most recent extraordinary three-year state aid package is earmarked for online initiatives.) These are just a few examples of new policy discussions bubbling up in different countries around the world, often pitting legacy players against new entrants like Google and forcing legal, regulatory, and legislative authorities to stretch old frameworks to cover new cases and to reconcile inherited norms and expectations surrounding for instance privacy protection, copyright, and fair use with rapid technological advances.

In the United Kingdom, many like to think of media policy-making there as more globally oriented than in France or Germany. And indeed the country is fortunate to have a relatively strong industry with several global players (including the BBC, Pearson, Thomson-Reuters and BSkyB/News Corporation to name a few). However the danger of the UK policy debate is that as it tries to address the current problems of the news industry it gets so bogged down in the familiar issue of the BBC versus the existing market players that it may miss some the larger global challenges posed by new players such as Google.

These debates and media policy more generally are no different from any other area of public policy in being riddled with ideological disputes, inherited ideas, conflicts of interests, and an absence of any outside arbiters of what is the best way forward for the business of journalism. What can be said, in any case, is that they demonstrate that there *are* things that can be done, different ways forward, and that some of them involve public policy – given the long history of state involvement with media policy, even in the United States, it thus seems like a remarkable failure of imagination when White House spokesman Robert Gibbs claims: 'I don't know what, in all honesty, government can do [to help journalism]' (Wilson 2009). As the contributors to this book have made clear, there are plenty of useful examples of public intervention and support from around the world. The French government at least has talked the talk – according to President Sarkozy, 'It is the state's primary responsibility to respond to an emergency, and there is an emergency [in the business of journalism] caused by the impact of the collapse of advertising revenue' (Pfanner 2009) – but, as Alice Antheaume has made clear in her chapter, it is finding it harder to walk the walk of substantial reform.

What's next?

We do not want to belittle the challenges ahead, the losses incurred by investors and owners, or the real human costs for the thousands of journalists who have lost their jobs in recent widespread layoffs. But it is important to keep in mind that there *are* ways ahead, that current transformations bring not only threats, but also opportunities. None of the evidence reviewed here suggests that the business of journalism has reached the end of the line, that the current crisis is terminal for the industry or the vocation it has sustained. All around the world, as in all the countries discussed in this book, new generations of managers and journalists are reinventing the business and the profession, and charitable foundations and governments are considering what role *they* can play in making sure professional journalism underwritten by privately profitable commercial news media can continue to play a publicly valuable role in our democracies. This is no time for fatalism.

When talk turns to how we carry into the twenty-first century the best of what the free and independent press of the twentieth century represented and claimed to represent, it is important not only to be clear-eyed about what commercial news organisations are and have been but also to ask ourselves what it is about them we are trying to sustain. Newspapers were never simply the valiant watchdogs of democracy celebrated in after-dinner speeches, but frequently also sensationalist, self-interested, and prejudiced, as pointed out by many critics. If we want to support their attempts to reinvent themselves, what is it we are trying to maintain? Their market value, the occupation they have employed, or a set of partially democratic practices developed partially within the industry? If it is simply a matter of commerce or jobs, newspapers hardly look 'too big to fail' – as Alan Mutter (2008) has pointed out; the industry generated only 0.36 per cent of the US Gross National Product and employed a mere 0.2 per cent of the labour force in 2008. The reason we worry more when the last news organisation closes than when the last furniture factory shuts down, is of course the important and imperfect diverse roles journalism plays and have played in our democracies.

Journalism has many relations, for good and for bad, to democracy. Michael Schudson listed no less than six things journalism can do for democracy in his contribution to this book (inform the public, keep an eye on the powerful, analyse and explain the world, encourage social empathy, constitute a public forum, and serve as advocates for social change). (See Schudson 2008 for a fuller treatment.) Journalism's unique ability to play these benign roles is sometimes exaggerated (as pointed out by Gans 2003), and they do not necessarily go hand-in-hand. (It is by no means a given, for example, that precisely professional journalism is the best available or most cost-effective way of maintaining a lively public debate, or that what is good for debate also makes for good news. Arguably, some of the very same technologies often blamed today for undermining the economic viability of the private press have done more to make vigorous, passionate, and participatory discussion possible than the letters pages ever did – see Benkler 2006; Dutton 2009.)

Throughout most of the twentieth century, commercial news organisations grew increasingly central, important, and powerful in most developed democracies – sometimes excessively so (Benkler 2006) – in particular as a source of information about public affairs, the first role mentioned by Schudson, and the one most of those who write about the relations between journalism and democracy focus on (Gans 2003; Keane 1991; Curran 2005). Especially in countries with weak public service media organisations, the private press and commercial television have occupied the commanding heights of our media systems, producing and providing most of the news consumed, making it possible for people to become more or less informed citizens.

The business of journalism was never alone in this – it was always surrounded by various forms of alternative or citizen journalism, embedded in informal networks of interpersonal communication, and other means of sharing information (libraries, etc.). It was never only underwritten by the business employing those behind the by-lines either, but also directly and indirectly through public policy and media regulation, through information subsidies from civil society organisations, research institutions, and government bodies, and often by the helpful hands willingly extended by PR professionals and the press offices of political parties and governments. But the business of journalism was undeniably central.

Today, this very same business of journalism is in crisis in some countries, and in a period of transition in most countries across the world, faced with cyclical, technological, and long-term challenges and operating in what seems to be an ever-expanding communications environment, where non-journalistic forms of content are multiplying at a vastly faster pace than news production. Commercial legacy news organisations will increasingly have to operate in systems characterised by abundance and increased competition, especially when it comes to general-interest news, political and personal opinions, and news and gossip about sports and entertainment. Their own role will probably often be diminished.

For those who subscribe to Christopher Lasch's notion that democracy does not need information as much as it needs public debate (Lasch 1990), and who think that other entities will fill the watchdog role, analyse and contextualise world affairs for us, foster social cohesion, and drive social change (or at least do more of this than journalism ever did), there seem to be few grounds to worry. Surely the viewspapers, cable channels, and blogging sites of today and tomorrow, and the offline coffee shops, personal peer groups, and online social networking sites where they are discussed, provide a more robust environment for participatory conversations than the hub-and-spoke mass media system of the mid- to late twentieth century.

But for those who believe that democracies work better when news supplements conversations, when there at least exists a common ground of publicly shared facts (whether people choose to operate on it or not), we have to hope that entrepreneurs amongst the business people, news professionals, and policy-makers who care about journalism find the key to unlocking the democratic potential of a new era of technologically enhanced journalism. Progress seems likely to rely on the market and civil society actors (and perhaps state support) to produce news and sustain journalism across all media platforms. The democratic role played by news requires journalism to serve the interests of the entire population and not only the business, the profession, and the most affluent and educated elites (Curran 2005; Gans 2003; Keane 1991). And yet it is precisely this notion of universal news that is where gaps may be most likely to open up when and if the business of journalism finds a way out of its current problems, in particular if exclusion comes to trump mutualisation and public access as the dominant commercial strategy.

It is today that we can establish the framework conditions, underlying infrastructure, and regulatory environment for the journalism of tomorrow. *Not* acting may be as consequential as taking deliberate and decisive action. It is no longer sufficient to simply reiterate that journalism is a public good and that we want a free and independent press. These are useful slogans, but they are starting points for a debate, not conclusions. What is needed today is to move on to a more serious discussion of (*a*) what sustainable balance can be found between the elements of journalism that are public goods and the rest of journalism, (*b*) how one can ensure the provision of those elements that truly are important for democracies and that the market alone is unlikely to deliver, (*c*) what mix of market, civil society, and public provision is then desirable, and (*d*) how the result can be made available – across any number of platforms – to the wider population who is supposed to benefit from it all, and in terms of whose interest intervention can be legitimised in the first place.

These are not questions to which there are definitive answers, but about which reasonable and principled disagreements exist and solutions are always open to debate. We hope, however, that media managers, professional journalists, policy-makers, and citizens who confront them will move beyond the journalism of yesterday and the national traditions they are familiar with and seek inspiration from each other and the wider world as they try to establish new business models and carve out a space for the journalism of the future.

References

AFP (2009) '"Mon journal offert": un abonnement gratuit pour les jeunes de 18–24 ans', 27 Oct.: www.google.com/hostednews/afp/article/ALeqM5inlm0Jz4Gh46BcMNdlI4u_f-AU2A (accessed Aug. 2010).

An, S., H. S. Jin, and T. Simon (2006) 'Ownership Structure of Publicly Traded Newspaper Companies and their Financial Performance', *Journal of Media Economics*, 19/2: 119.

Axel Springer (2010) 'Hamburg Declaration regarding intellectual property rights': www.axelspringer.de/downloads/153453/Hamburg_Declaration.pdf (accessed Aug. 2010).

Bakker, G. (2010) 'The Economic History of the International Film Industry'. EH.net (Economic History Association): http://eh.net/encyclopedia/article/bakker.film (accessed Aug. 2010).

Barnett, S. (2002) 'Will a Crisis in Journalism Provoke a Crisis in Democracy?', *Political Quarterly*, 73/4: 400–8.

Benkler, Y. (2006) *The Wealth of Networks: How Social Production Transforms Markets and Freedom*. New Haven, Conn.: Yale University Press.

Bennett, W. L., R. G. Lawrence, and S. Livingston (2007) *When the Press Fails: Political Power and the News Media from Iraq to Katrina*. Chicago: University of Chicago Press.

Coleman, S., S. Anthony, and D. E. Morrison (2009) *Public Trust in the News: A Constructivist Study of the Social Life of the News*. Oxford: Reuters Institute for the Study of Journalism.

Curran, J. (2005) 'Mediations of Democracy', in J. Curran and M. Gurevitch, *Mass Media and Society*, 4th edn. London: Hodder Arnold, 122–49.

Dutton, W. H. (2009) 'The Fifth Estate Emerging through the Network of Networks', *Prometheus: Critical Studies in Innovation*, 27/1: 1.

Gans, H. J. (2003) *Democracy and the News* Oxford: Oxford University Press.

Gardam, T., and D. A. L. Levy, eds (2008) *The Price of Plurality: Choice, Diversity and Broadcasting Institutions in the Digital Age*. Oxford: Reuters Institute for the Study of Journalism.

Goldman, D. (2010) 'Music's Lost Decade: Sales Cut in Half', *CNN Money*, 3 Feb.: http://money.cnn.com/2010/02/02/news/companies/napster_music_industry/index.htm (accessed Aug. 2010).

Hacker, J. S. (2004) 'Privatizing Risk without Privatizing the Welfare State: The Hidden Politics of Social Policy Retrenchment in the United States', *American Political*

Science Review, 98/2: 243–60.

Jarvis, J. (2009) 'The Half Life of News': www.buzzmachine.com/2009/11/23/the-half-life-of-news/ (accessed Aug. 2010).

Jones, D. A. (2004) 'Why Americans Don't Trust the Media', *Harvard International Journal of Press/Politics*, 9/2: 60–75.

Keane, J. (1991) *The Media and Democracy*. Cambridge: Polity Press.

Lasch, C. (1990) 'Journalism, Publicity and the Lost Art of Argument', *Gannett Center Journal* (Spring): 1–11.

Murdoch, J. (2009) 'The Absence of Trust': www.broadcastnow.co.uk/comment/james-murdochs-mactaggart-speech/5004990.article (accessed Aug. 2010).

Mutter, A. (2008) 'Why Feds Won't Bail Out Newspapers': http://newsosaur.blogspot.com/2008/11/why-feds-wont-bail-out-newspapers.html (accessed Aug. 2010).

OECD (2010) *The Evolution of News and the Internet*. Paris: OECD.

Pew Project for Excellence in Journalism (2010) *The State of the News Media 2010*. New York: Journalism.org. Available at: www.stateofthenewsmedia.org/2010.

Pfanner, E. (2009) 'France to Aid Newspapers', *New York Times* (23 Jan.): www.nytimes.com/2009/01/23/business/worldbusiness/23iht-ads.4.19637222.html?scp=1&sq=sarkozy%20newspapers&st=cse (accessed Aug. 2010).

Pickard, V., J. Stearns, and C. Aaron (2009) *Saving the News*. Washington, DC: Free Press: www.freepress.net/files/saving_the_news.pdf (accessed Aug. 2010).

Rusbridger, A. (2009) 'I've Seen the Future and it's Mutual', *British Journalism Review*, 20/3: 19–26.

Schudson, M. (2008) *Why Democracies Need an Unlovable Press*. Cambridge: Polity.

— (2010) '"The Reconstruction of American Journalism" and Beyond': http://reutersinstitute.politics.ox.ac.uk/fileadmin/documents/Conferences/Reconstruction_of_American_Journalism/The_Reconstruction of_American_Journalism_-_Schudson_speech.pdf (accessed Aug. 2010).

Shirky, C. (2009) 'Newspapers and Thinking the Unthinkable': www.shirky.com/weblog/2009/03/newspapers and thinking-the-unthinkable (accessed Jan. 2010).

Starr, P. (2004) *The Creation of the Media: Political Origins of Modern Communications*. New York: Basic Books.

Thelen, K. (1999) 'Historical Institutionalism in Comparative Politics', *Annual Review of Political Science*, 2/1: 369–404.

Wilson, S. (2009) 'Gibbs: No Newspaper Bailout from Government', *Washington Post* (4 May): http://voices.washingtonpost.com/44/2009/05/04/gibbs_no_newspaper_bailout_fro.html?hpid=topnews (accessed Aug. 2010).

List of contributors

ALICE ANTHEAUME is Associate Director of the Journalism School at Sciences Po (Paris), France

MICHAEL BRÜGGEMANN is Oberassistent at Institut für Publizistikwissenschaft und Medienforschung (IPMZ) at the University of Zürich, Switzerland.

FRANK ESSER is Professor of International and Comparative Media Research at Institut für Publizistikwissenschaft und Medienforschung (IPMZ) at the University of Zürich, Switzerland.

DAVID A. L. LEVY is Director of the Reuters Institute for the Study of Journalism and an Associate Fellow of the Saïd Business School, University of Oxford.

JOHN LLOYD is Director of Journalism at the Reuters Institute for the Study of Journalism, University of Oxford. and a Contributing Editor to the *Financial Times*.

RASMUS KLEIS NIELSEN is a Research Fellow at the Reuters Institute for the Study of Journalism, University of Oxford.

HANNU NIEMINEN is Professor of Media and Communication Policy and Director of the Communication Research Centre (CRC) at the University of Helsinki, Finland.

ROBERT G. PICARD is Director of Research at the Reuters Institute for the Study of Journalism, University of Oxford, and editor of the *Journal of Media Business Studies*.

MAURO PORTO is Assistant Professor in the Department of Communication, Tulane University, USA, and about to take up a position as Program Officer of Media Rights and Access at the Ford Foundation headquarters in Rio de Janeiro, Brazil.

MICHAEL SCHUDSON is Professor at the Graduate School of Journalism and Professor (Courtesy) of Sociology at Columbia University, USA.

DAYA KISHAN THUSSU is Professor of International Communication and Co-Director of India Media Centre at the University of Westminster.

SACHA WUNSCH-VINCENT wrote this chapter in his former capacity as Senior Economist at the OECD and author of their 2010 study *The Evolution of News and the Internet*.